Directed Reading A

Section: The Rock Cycle

______ **1.** A naturally occurring solid mixture of one or more minerals or organic matter is called
   a. an element.
   b. a rock.
   c. a compound.
   d. an atom.

______ **2.** The continual process by which new rock forms from old rock is called
   a. deposition.
   b. erosion.
   c. the rock cycle.
   d. compaction.

THE VALUE OF ROCK

3. Rocks have been used by humans throughout history for tools, weapons,

and _______________________.

ROUND AND ROUND IT GOES

______ **4.** Which of the following forces affects rock deep beneath Earth's surface?
   a. pressure
   b. erosion
   c. weathering
   d. deposition

______ **5.** A rock at the earth's surface is primarily affected by forces of
   a. heat and pressure.
   b. pressure only.
   c. weathering and erosion.
   d. cooling.

Directed Reading A *continued*

_______ **6.** A rock deep underground is primarily affected by forces of
    a. extreme heat and pressure.
    b. cooling.
    c. weathering and erosion.
    d. heat only.

_______ **7.** What kind of new material is formed when metamorphic rock melts?
    a. igneous rock
    b. sedimentary rock
    c. metamorphic rock
    d. magma

_______ **8.** What kind of new rock is formed when igneous rock is subjected to weathering, erosion, compaction, and cementation?
    a. magma
    b. sedimentary rock
    c. metamorphic rock
    d. igneous rock

_______ **9.** What new kind of rock is formed when sedimentary rock is subjected to heat and pressure?
    a. igneous rock
    b. sedimentary rock
    c. metamorphic rock
    d. magma

ILLUSTRATING THE ROCK CYCLE

Match the correct description with the correct term. Write the letter in the space provided.

_______**10.** magma in the Earth's crust that has risen to the surface and cools and solidifies

_______**11.** rock that is forced downward and is exposed to heat and pressure

_______**12.** rocks that are partially or completely melted

_______**13.** igneous rock at the Earth's surface that is weathered and wears away

_______**14.** sediment that washes down into rivers and oceans and is pressed and cemented together

a. magma

b. sediment

c. igneous rock

d. sedimentary rock

e. metamorphic rock

Directed Reading A *continued*

PROCESSES THAT SHAPE THE EARTH

15. The process in which water, wind, ice, and heat break down rock is

called _____________________________.

16. One reason that weathering is important is because it breaks rock down into

fragments, or _____________________________, from which sedimentary rocks
are made.

17. The process by which sediment is removed from its source is

called _____________________________.

18. During _____________________________, sediment is deposited in bodies of water
and other low-lying areas.

19. Sedimentary rock can be made when sediment is pressed and cemented

together by _____________________________ dissolved in water.

20. Some _____________________________ rock is made when sediment is squeezed by
the weight of the rock materials that lies above it.

21. Movement within the Earth that causes buried rock to be exposed at the

Earth's surface is called _____________________________.

22. When uplifted rocks reach _____________________________, weathering, erosion,
and deposition begin.

ROCK CLASSIFICATION

_______**23.** Beyond the three basic types of rock, rocks can be divided into
subcategories based on
a. composition and texture.
b. the depth at which they formed.
c. elevation.
d. the pressure under which they formed.

_______**24.** What is the chemical makeup, or mineral content, of a rock based on?
a. the size of its grains
b. the positions of its grains
c. the shape of its grains
d. its composition

Directed Reading A *continued*

_______**25.** A rock that consists mostly of the mineral quartz will have a composition very similar to
   a. basalt.
   b. siltstone.
   c. quartz.
   d. sandstone.

_______**26.** What do the size, shape, and positions of the grains that make up a rock determine?
   a. the rock's texture
   b. the rock's size
   c. the rock's color
   d. the rock's composition

_______**27.** What factors can affect the texture of a sedimentary rock?
   a. the length of time the magma had to cool
   b. the temperature the rock was exposed to
   c. the color of the rock
   d. the size of the grains that make up the rock

_______**28.** What factors can affect the texture of an igneous rock?
   a. the length of time the magma had to cool
   b. the size of the rock
   c. the minerals that cement the rock together
   d. the pressure and temperature the rock was exposed to

_______**29.** What factor can affect the texture of a metamorphic rock?
   a. the length of time the magma had to cool
   b. the pressure and temperature the rock was exposed to
   c. the minerals that cement the rock together
   d. the size of the grains that make up the rock

Directed Reading A

Section: Igneous Rock

_______ **1.** What kind of rock forms when hot, liquid rock, or magma, cools and solidifies?
   a. sedimentary
   b. igneous
   c. metamorphic
   d. mineral

_______ **2.** Which kind of rock has a name that comes from a Latin word that means "fire"?
   a. igneous
   b. metamorphic
   c. metasedimentary
   d. sedimentary

3. What two factors affect the type of igneous rock that is formed?

____

____

ORIGINS OF IGNEOUS ROCK

4. The material that igneous rock is made up of is

called _______________________.

5. What are the three ways that magma can form?

____

____

____

6. What three factors affect the formation of magma?

____

____

____

7. How does the composition of the magma affect the temperature at which it solidifies?

____

____

Directed Reading A *continued*

COMPOSITION AND TEXTURE OF IGNEOUS ROCK

8. Light-colored igneous rocks are less _________________ than dark-colored igneous rocks are.

9. Light-colored igneous rocks that are rich in aluminum, potassium, silicon and sodium are called _________________.

10. Dark-colored igneous rocks that are rich in calcium, iron, and magnesium are called _________________.

11. The longer it takes for a rock to cool and solidify, the more time _________________ have to grow, giving the rock a(n) _________________ grain.

12. The more quickly an igneous rock cools and solidifies, the _________________ the grain.

13. The igneous rock that has cooled most quickly will be found on the _________________ of a volcano.

IGNEOUS ROCK FORMATIONS

Match the correct description with the correct term. Write the letter in the space provided.

_______**14.** rock that forms below the earth's surface

_______**15.** a large, irregular-shaped intrusive body

_______**16.** the largest intrusive bodies

_______**17.** sheetlike intrusions that lie parallel to previous rock units

_______**18.** sheetlike intrusions that cut across previous rock units

a. pluton

b. dikes

c. batholiths

d. intrusive igneous rock

e. sills

19. Magma _________________, or pushes, into surrounding rock below the Earth's surface to create such formations as batholiths and sills.

20. Intrusive igneous rock usually has a(n) _________________ texture.

21. Igneous rock that forms from lava, or magma that erupts onto the Earth's surface, is called _________________.

Directed Reading A *continued*

22. Lava can either erupt or flow from long cracks in the Earth's crust

called _________________________.

23. When lava flows from fissures on the ocean floor at places where tension is

causing the ocean floor to be pulled apart, new _________________________
is formed.

24. When a large amount of lava flows out of fissures onto land, the lava can

cover a large area and form a plain called a(n) _________________________.

Directed Reading A

Section: Sedimentary Rock

1. Over time, grains of sand may be compacted and cemented together to form a

rock called _____________________.

ORIGINS OF SEDIMENTARY ROCK

2. When sediment is deposited in layers and

compacted, _____________________ is formed.

3. Dissolved minerals separate from water and become a

natural _____________________ that binds the sedimentary rock together.

4. Sedimentary rocks form at or near the Earth's _____________________.

5. The most noticeable feature of sedimentary rock is often its layers,

or _____________________.

COMPOSITION OF SEDIMENTARY ROCK

6. Rock or mineral fragments are called _____________________.

7. Sedimentary rock that forms when rock or mineral fragments are cemented

together is called _____________________ sedimentary rock.

8. Clastic sedimentary rocks can have coarse-, medium-, or

fine-grained _____________________.

9. Sedimentary rock that forms when minerals crystallize out of solution, such

as sea water, to become rock is called _____________________
sedimentary rock.

10. Sedimentary rock that forms from the remains, or fossils, of plants and

animals is called _____________________ sedimentary rock.

11. Some limestone is made from the skeletons of tiny _____________________

that live in the ocean in huge colonies called _____________________.

12. Limestone made from the calcium carbonate from skeletons and shells of sea

creatures is called _____________________ limestone.

| Directed Reading A *continued*

13. An organic sedimentary rock that forms from the action of heat and pressure

on plant material over millions of years is called __________________.

SEDIMENTARY ROCK STRUCTURES

_______**14.** What is the process in which sedimentary rocks are arranged in
layers?
- **a.** mud cracking
- **b.** weathering
- **c.** stratification
- **d.** erosion

_______**15.** What are the markings on sedimentary rocks that record the wave
motion of wind or water called?
- **a.** ripple marks
- **b.** stratification
- **c.** fossiliferous limestone
- **d.** mud cracks

_______**16.** What do we call the structures that form when fine-grained sediments
at the bottom of a shallow body of water are exposed to the air and
dry out?
- **a.** ripple marks
- **b.** fossiliferous limestone
- **c.** coal
- **d.** mud cracks

_______**17.** Which sedimentary rock type most likely formed from ancient sand
dunes?
- **a.** clastic sedimentary rock
- **b.** fossiliferous limestone
- **c.** chemical sedimentary rock
- **d.** organic sedimentary rock

Directed Reading A

Section: Metamorphic Rock

_______ **1.** Which rock's name comes from the Greek words for "changed" and "shape"?
  a. metamorphic
  b. sedimentary
  c. fossiliferous limestone
  d. igneous

_______ **2.** What kind of rocks are rocks in which the structure, texture, or composition have been changed?
  a. fossiliferous limestone
  b. igneous
  c. metamorphic
  d. sedimentary

_______ **3.** What force or forces can create metamorphic rocks?
  a. cooling
  b. heat and pressure
  c. melting
  d. erosion

ORIGINS OF METAMORPHIC ROCK

4. The heat and pressure at which some metamorphic rocks originally form allow them to sometimes remain _____________________ at pressures and temperatures that would melt other rock.

5. Pressure caused by large movements within the crust sometimes cause the _____________________ in metamorphic rocks to align themselves in parallel bands.

6. During _____________________, rock is heated by nearby magma.

7. The effect of heat on rock decreases as the rock's _____________________ from the magma increases and its _____________________ decreases.

8. When pressure builds up in rock which is located under other rock formations, _____________________ occurs.

9. Regional metamorphism occurs deep in the Earth's _____________________.

| Directed Reading A *continued*

COMPOSITION OF METAMORPHIC ROCK

______**10.** Which of the following is NOT a property of an index mineral?
    a. forms only at a certain temperature
    b. forms only in sedimentary rock
    c. forms only at certain temperatures
    d. forms only in metamorphic rocks

______**11.** Which of the following minerals is an example of an index mineral?
    a. calcite
    b. quartz
    c. staurolite
    d. hematite

______**12.** Which of the following is an example of a mineral that indicates that a metamorphic rock was formed at a great depth and under extreme heat and pressure?
    a. chlorite
    b. mica
    c. magma
    d. garnet

TEXTURES OF METAMORPHIC ROCK

______**13.** What do we call metamorphic rocks in which mineral grains are NOT aligned?
    a. foliated
    b. intrusive
    c. nonfoliated
    d. extrusive

______**14.** What is the process in which a mineral changes composition during metamorphism called?
    a. recrystallization
    b. nonfoliation
    c. foliation
    d. deformation

______**15.** After quartz limestone has recrystallized, the new rock is called
    a. schist.
    b. gneiss.
    c. slate.
    d. quartzite.

| Directed Reading A *continued*

Match the correct description with the correct term. Write the letter in the space provided.

________16. a rock in which coarse-grained minerals separate into distinct bands

________17. a foliated metamorphic rock made from shale

________18. a metamorphic rock with mineral grains in planes or bands

________19. a metamorphic rock made from phyllite that has been exposed to heat and pressure

________20. a sedimentary rock made of layers of clay

________21. a metamorphic rock made from slate that has been subjected to heat and pressure

a. foliated

b. shale

c. slate

d. phyllite

e. schist

f. gneiss

METAMORPHIC ROCK STRUCTURES

________22. What is a change in the shape of a rock caused by a force placed on it called?
   a. deformation
   b. recrystallization
   c. foliation
   d. nonfoliation

Directed Reading B

Section: The Rock Cycle

<u>Circle the letter</u> of the best answer for each question.

1. What is a solid mixture of one or more minerals and organic matter called?

   a. sediment

   b. sand

   c. rock

   d. magma

2. What is the process called that forms new rock from old rock?

   a. the erosion cycle

   b. the rock cycle

   c. the water cycle

   d. the carbon cycle

THE VALUE OF ROCK

3. Early humans made arrowheads from which rock?

   a. chert

   b. marble

   c. sandstone

   d. limestone

PROCESSES THAT SHAPE THE EARTH

Weathering, Erosion, and Deposition

<u>Circle the letter</u> of the best answer for each question.

4. What moves sediment from one place to another?

   a. deposition

   b. weathering

   c. erosion

   d. uplift

Directed Reading B *continued*

Circle the letter of the best answer for each question.

5. What is it called when sediment is deposited in a body of water?

  a. deposition

  b. uplift

  c. weathering

  d. erosion

Heat and Pressure

6. What rock forms when sediment is squeezed by the weight of the rock above it?

  a. igneous rock

  b. sedimentary rock

  c. metasedimentary rock

  d. metamorphic rock

How the Cycle Continues

7. Besides erosion, what else causes rock to be expose at the Earth's surface?

  a. uplift

  b. compaction

  c. deposition

  d. cementation

ROUND AND ROUND IT GOES

8. In the rock cycle, which factor determines which forces will change a rock?

  a. location

  b. heat

  c. pressure

  d. time

| **Directed Reading B** *continued*

Circle the letter of the best answer for each question.

9. What forces work on rocks at Earth's surface?

    a. heat and pressure

    b. pressure and erosion

    c. compaction and cementation

    d. melting and cooling

10. What affects rocks inside the Earth?

    a. heat and pressure

    b. weathering

    c. erosion

    d. deposition

11. What material is formed when metamorphic rock melts?

    a. igneous rock

    b. sedimentary rock

    c. metamorphic rock

    d. magma

12. What kind of rock is formed by the weathering and erosion of igneous rocks?

    a. magma

    b. sedimentary rock

    c. metamorphic rock

    d. igneous rock

13. What kind of rock is formed when sedimentary rock is subjected to heat and pressure?

    a. igneous rock

    b. sedimentary rock

    c. metamorphic rock

    d. magma

ILLUSTRATING THE ROCK CYCLE

Read the words in the box. Read the sentences. <u>Fill in each blank</u> with the word or phrase that best completes the sentence.

magma	deposition
sediment	weathering

14. During ___________________________, sediment is deposited in

bodies of water.

15. The process in which water, wind, ice, and heat break down rock

is called ___________________________.

16. Weathering breaks down rock into fragments, or

___________________________, from which sedimentary rocks

are made.

17. Because ___________________________ is less dense than

surrounding rock, it rises.

ROCK CLASSIFICATION

18. Which of the following is not one of the three main classes of rock?

    a. igneous rock   **c.** sedimentary rock

    b. volcanic rock   **d.** metamorphic rock

19. How do scientists classify rocks?

    a. by color   **c.** by mass

    b. by volume   **d.** by composition and texture

Composition

20. What is meant by the composition of a rock?

    a. chemical makeup   **c.** grain size

    b. grain shape   **d.** grain positions

| Directed Reading B *continued*

● **Texture**

<u>Circle the letter</u> of the best answer for each question.

21. Besides size and position, what else determines clastic sedimentary rock texture?

a. temperature of the grains

b. length of the grains

c. width of the grains

d. shape of the grains

22. What type of grains determine clastic sedimentary rock texture?

a. round and square   **c.** small, medium, and large

b. fine, medium, and coarse   **d.** heavy and light

23. Which rock's texture is determined by the size of the grains?

a. igneous

b. metamorphic

c. metasedimentary

d. sedimentary

24. Which rock's texture is determined by how fast the magma cooled?

a. igneous

b. metamorphic

c. metasedimentary

d. sedimentary

25. Which rock's texture is determined by the pressure and temperature the rock was exposed to?

a. metasedimentary

b. metamorphic

c. igneous

d. sedimentary

Directed Reading B

Section: Igneous Rock

Circle the letter of the best answer for each question.

1. How are igneous rocks formed?

    a. when magma cools and solidifies

    b. when sediments are compacted and cemented

    c. when heat and pressure squeezes rock

    d. when rocks are deformed

ORIGINS OF IGNEOUS ROCK

2. What is one way that magma can form?

    a. when rock is cooled   **c.** when rock is weathered

    b. when rock is cemented   **d.** when rock is heated

3. Besides pressure being released, what other way can magma form?

    a. when pressure builds up   **c.** when rocks change composition

    b. when rocks solidify   **d.** when rocks lose water

4. When magma cools, what does it form?

    a. more magma   **c.** sedimentary rock

    b. igneous rock   **d.** metamorphic rock

5. At what temperature does magma solidify?

    a. between 70°C and 125°C   **c.** at 0°C

    b. at 32°F   **d.** between 700°C and 1,250°C

6. Because minerals found in magma have different melting points,

    a. some minerals become solid before others.

    b. some minerals never solidify.

    c. some minerals never melt.

    d. all minerals solidify at the same temperature.

| Directed Reading B *continued*

COMPOSITION AND TEXTURE OF IGNEOUS ROCK

Read the words in the box. Read the sentences. <u>Fill in each blank</u> with the word or phrase that best completes the sentence.

felsic rocks	fine	cooled
mafic rocks	crystals	

7. The more time the _______________________ have to grow, the larger and coarser the texture is.

8. Aluminum, potassium, silicon, and sodium make light-colored rocks called _______________________.

9. Dark-colored rocks called _______________________ have more calcium, iron, and magnesium.

10. Igneous rocks differ from one another in how fast they _______________________.

11. Igneous rocks that have small crystals have _______________________ grains.

IGNEOUS ROCK FORMATIONS

<u>Circle the letter</u> of the best answer for each question.

12. Intrusive igneous rock usually has what kind of texture?

    a. coarse-grained   **c.** small-grained

    b. medium-grained   **d.** fine-grained

Intrusive Igneous Rock

13. What is a sheetlike intrusion that is oriented parallel to previous rock layers called?

    a. a stock   **c.** a dike

    b. a batholith   **d.** a sill

Directed Reading B *continued*

Circle the letter of the best answer for each question.

14. What are large, irregular-shaped intrusive bodies called?

   a. stocks

   b. plutons

   c. sills

   d. dikes

15. What are the largest igneous intrusions called?

   a. dikes

   b. stocks

   c. batholiths

   d. sills

Extrusive Igneous Rock

16. What is it called when magma erupts on the Earth's surface?

   a. intrusive igneous rock

   b. metamorphic rock

   c. sedimentary rock

   d. extrusive igneous rock

17. Besides volcanoes, where else does lava flow from?

   a. fissures

   b. sills

   c. plateaus

   d. batholiths

18. What landform is created when lava flows out of a fissure onto land?

   a. a rolling hill

   b. a lava plateau

   c. a tall mountain

   d. a volcanic neck

Directed Reading B

Section: Sedimentary Rock
ORIGINS OF SEDIMENTARY ROCK

Read the words in the box. Read the sentences. <u>Fill in each blank</u> with the word or phrase that best completes the sentence.

strata	sediment	dissolved minerals
erosion	weather	surface

1. Wind, water, ice and gravity cause rock to

_______________________________ into fragments.

2. Fragments of rock are called _______________________________.

3. Sediment moves from one place to another during the process of

_______________________________.

4. When new layers of _______________________________ are deposited,

they cover older layers.

5. Cement made from _______________________________ binds the

fragments together.

6. The most noticeable feature of sedimentary rocks are their layers

called _______________________________.

Directed Reading B *continued*

COMPOSITION OF SEDIMENTARY ROCK

Read the description. Then, <u>draw a line</u> from the dot next to each description to the matching word.

7. rock that forms when minerals crystallize out of a solution •

8. rock that forms from the remains of plants and animals •

9. rock or mineral fragments •

10. rock that forms when clasts are cemented together •

a. clastic sedimentary rock

b. clasts

c. chemical sedimentary rock

d. organic sedimentary rock

Clastic Sedimentary Rock

<u>Circle the letter</u> of the best answer for each question.

11. How are clastic sedimentary rocks classified?

    a. mineral shape

    b. fragment shape

    c. fragment size

    d. mineral size

Chemical Sedimentary Rock

12. Which of the following is a chemical sedimentary rock?

    a. conglomerate

    b. coal

    c. halite

    d. shale

Directed Reading B *continued*

Circle the letter of the best answer for each question.

13. What does chemical sedimentary rock form from?

    a. minerals that crystallize out of solution

    b. clasts

    c. decomposed plant material

    d. fossils

14. What is the chemical makeup of halite?

    a. calcium carbonate

    b. silicon dioxide

    c. calcium sulfate

    d. sodium chloride

Organic Sedimentary Rock

Read the words in the box. Read the sentences. Fill in each blank with the word or phrase that best completes the sentence.

coral	coal	fossiliferous limestone
fossils	reefs	

15. Limestone can be formed from _______________________________, or

the remains of animals.

16. Some limestone is formed from the skeletons of tiny organisms

called _______________________________.

17. Coral live in huge underwater colonies called

_______________________________.

18. Animal remains that are cemented together can form

_______________________________.

19. Decomposed plant material under the ground makes

_______________________________.

Directed Reading B *continued*

SEDIMENTARY ROCK STRUCTURES
Circle the letter of the best answer for each question.

20. What is the process in which sedimentary rocks are arranged in layers?

    a. cementation

    b. stratification

    c. crystallization

    d. erosion

21. What are the markings on sedimentary rocks that record the waves of wind and water?

    a. strata

    b. shorelines

    c. mud cracks

    d. ripple marks

22. What sedimentary structure indicates the location of an ancient shoreline?

    a. ripple marks

    b. mud cracks

    c. strata

    d. fissures

Skills Worksheet

Directed Reading B

Section: Metamorphic Rock
ORIGINS OF METAMORPHIC ROCK

Circle the letter of the best answer for each question.

1. What process is a rock undergoing when the new environment is different from the one in which the rock was formed?

   a. erosion

   b. melting

   c. metamorphism

   d. deposition

2. What kind of rocks can remain solid at temperatures and pressures that would melt other rocks?

   a. intrusive igneous

   b. metamorphic

   c. extrusive igneous

   d. sedimentary

3. What aligns in parallel bands due to added pressure on a rock during metamorphism?

   a. mineral grains

   b. sediment

   c. clasts

   d. fossils

Contact Metamorphism

4. What occurs when a rock undergoes metamorphism by being heated by nearby magma?

   a. erosion

   b. deposition

   c. regional metamorphism

   d. contact metamorphism

| Directed Reading B *continued*

Circle the letter of the best answer for each question.

5. The effect of contact metamorphism is greatest when the rock comes in direct contact with what?

a. water

b. magma

c. sediment

d. soil

Regional Metamorphism

6. What deforms and chemically changes rocks by means of increases in pressure and temperature?

a. erosion

b. contact metamorphism

c. regional metamorphism

d. deposition

7. What kind of metamorphism occurs over large areas deep in the Earth's crust?

a. regional metamorphism

b. erosion

c. contact metamorphism

d. deposition

Directed Reading B *continued*

COMPOSITION OF METAMORPHIC ROCK

Read the words in the box. Read the sentences. <u>Fill in each blank</u> with the word or phrase that best completes the sentence.

stable	index minerals	pressure

8. Metamorphism occurs when temperature and

_________________________________ inside the Earth's crust change.

9. During metamorphism, the original minerals change into minerals

that are _________________________ in the new conditions.

10. The presence of _____________________________ indicates the

temperature, pressure, and depth of rocks that undergo

metamorphism.

TEXTURES OF METAMORPHIC ROCK

Foliated Metamorphic Rock

Read the description. Then, <u>draw a line</u> from the dot next to each description to the matching word.

11. minerals grains that are arranged in bands ●

12. under pressure, shale becomes this ●

    a. slate

13. this rock forms when slate is exposed to ●
more heat and pressure

    b. gneiss

    c. foliated

14. schist exposed to more heat and pressure ●   **d.** phyllite
becomes this

Directed Reading B *continued*

Nonfoliated Metamorphic Rock
Circle the letter of the best answer for each question.

15. What do we call metamorphic rocks in which mineral grains are not arranged in bands?

a. slate

b. foliated

c. nonfoliated

d. gneiss

16. What do we call the process in which crystals change in size or composition?

a. foliation

b. recrystallization

c. sedimentation

d. deformation

17. What forms when quartz sandstone is exposed to heat and pressure?

a. phyllite

b. gneiss

c. shale

d. quartzite

Metamorphic Rock Structures

18. What is the term that describes the change in the shape of rock caused by squeezing or stretching?

a. cementation

b. metamorphism

c. recrystallization

d. deformation

19. What do folds and bends in rocks show?

a. They have been weathered.

b. They have been deformed.

c. They have been eroded.

d. They have been melted.

Vocabulary and Section Summary

The Rock Cycle

VOCABULARY

In your own words, write a definition of the following terms in the space provided.

1. rock cycle

____

____

2. rock

____

____

3. erosion

____

____

4. deposition

____

____

5. composition

____

____

6. texture

____

____

Vocabulary and Section Summary *continued*

SECTION SUMMARY

Read the following section summary.

- Rock has been an important natural resource for as long as humans have existed. Early humans used rock to make tools. Ancient and modern civilizations have used rock as a construction material.

- Weathering, erosion, deposition, and uplift are all processes that shape the surface features of the Earth.

- The rock cycle is the continual process by which new rock forms from old rock material. The sequence of events in the rock cycle depends on processes such as weathering, erosion, deposition, pressure, and heat that change the rock material.

- Composition and texture are two characteristics that scientists use to classify rocks.

- The composition of a rock is determined by the minerals that make up the rock.

- The texture of a rock is determined by the size, shape, and positions of the grains that make up the rock.

Skills Worksheet

Vocabulary and Section Summary

Igneous Rock

VOCABULARY

In your own words, write a definition of the following terms in the space provided.

1. intrusive igneous rock

____

____

2. extrusive igneous rock

____

____

SECTION SUMMARY

Read the following section summary.

- Igneous rock forms when magma cools and hardens.
- The texture of igneous rock is determined by the rate at which the rock cools.
- Igneous rock that solidifies at Earth's surface is extrusive. Igneous rock that solidifies within Earth's surface is intrusive.
- Shapes of common igneous intrusive bodies include batholiths, stocks, sills, and dikes.

Vocabulary and Section Summary

Sedimentary Rock

VOCABULARY

In your own words, write a definition of the following terms in the space provided.

1. strata

____

____

2. stratification

____

____

SECTION SUMMARY

Read the following section summary.

- Sedimentary rock forms at or near the Earth's surface.
- Clastic sedimentary rock forms when rock or mineral fragments are cemented together.
- Chemical sedimentary rock forms from solutions of dissolved minerals and water.
- Organic limestone forms from the remains of plants and animals.
- Sedimentary structures include ripple marks, mud cracks, and raindrop impressions

Vocabulary and Section Summary

Metamorphic Rock

VOCABULARY

In your own words, write a definition of the following terms in the space provided.

1. foliated

____

____

2. nonfoliated

____

____

SECTION SUMMARY

Read the following section summary.

- Metamorphic rocks are rocks in which the structure, texture, or composition has changed.

- Two ways rocks can undergo metamorphism are by contact metamorphism and regional metamorphism.

- As rocks undergo metamorphism, the original minerals in a rock change into new minerals that are more stable in new pressure and temperature conditions.

- Foliated metamorphic rock has mineral crystals aligned in planes or bands, whereas nonfoliated rocks have their mineral crystals unaligned.

- Metamorphic rock structures are caused by deformation.

Section Review

The Rock Cycle

USING KEY TERMS

Complete each of the following sentences by choosing the correct term from the word bank.

rock   composition

rock cycle   texture

1. The minerals that a rock is made of determine the _________________ of that rock.

2. _________________ is a naturally occurring solid mixture of one or more minerals and organic matter.

UNDERSTANDING KEY IDEAS

_______ **3.** Sediments are transported or moved from their original source by a process called

    a. deposition.

    b. erosion.

    c. uplift.

    d. weathering.

4. Describe two ways that rocks have been used by humans.

____

____

5. Name four processes that change rock inside the Earth.

____

____

____

____

6. Describe four processes that shape Earth's surface.

____

____

____

____

Section Review *continued*

7. Give an example of how texture can provide clues as to how and where a rock formed.

____

____

CRITICAL THINKING

8. Making Comparisons Explain the difference between texture and composition.

____

____

____

____

9. Analyzing Processes Explain how rock is continually recycled in the rock cycle.

____

____

____

____

INTERPRETING GRAPHICS

10. Look at the table below. Sandstone is a type of sedimentary rock. If you had a sample of sandstone that had an average particle size of 2 mm, what kind of texture would your sandstone have?

Classification of Clastic Sedimentary Rocks		
Texture	Particle Size	Main Constituents
coarse grained	> 2 mm	rock fragments, quartz
medium grained	0.06 to 2 mm	quartz, feldspar, rock fragments
fine grained	< 0.06 mm	clay minerals, quartz

____

____

____

Skills Worksheet

Section Review

Igneous Rock

USING KEY TERMS

1. In your own words, write a definition for each of the following terms: *intrusive igneous rock* and *extrusive igneous rock*.

____

____

____

____

UNDERSTANDING KEY IDEAS

2. _______ is an example of a coarse-grained, felsic, igneous rock.
   a. Basalt
   b. Gabbro
   c. Granite
   d. Rhyolite

3. Explain three ways in which magma can form.

____

____

____

4. What determines the texture of igneous rocks?

____

____

____

____

MATH SKILLS

5. The summit of a granite batholith has an elevation of 1,825 ft. What is the
height of the batholith in meters? Show your work below.

CRITICAL THINKING

6. Making Comparisons Dikes and sills are both types of igneous intrusive
bodies. What is the difference between a dike and a sill?

____

____

____

____

7. Predicting Consequences An igneous rock forms from slow-cooling magma
deep beneath the surface of the Earth? What type of texture is this rock most
likely to have? Explain.

____

____

____

____

Section Review

Sedimentary Rock

USING KEY TERMS

1. In your own words, write a definition for each of the following terms: *strata* and *stratification*.

UNDERSTANDING KEY IDEAS

______ 2. Which of the following is an organic sedimentary rock?
- **a.** chemical limestone
- **b.** shale
- **c.** fossiliferous limestone
- **d.** conglomerate

3. Explain the process by which sedimentary rock forms.

4. Describe the three main categories of sedimentary rock.

MATH SKILLS

5. A layer of a sedimentary rock is 2 m thick. How many years did it take for this layer to form if an average of 4 mm of sediment accumulated per year? Show your work below.

CRITICAL THINKING

6. Identifying Relationships Rocks are classified based on texture and composition. Which of these two properties would be more important for classifying clastic sedimentary rock?

____

____

____

____

7. Analyzing Processes Why do you think raindrop impressions are more likely to be preserved in fine-grained sedimentary rock rather than coarse-grained sedimentary rock?

____

____

____

____

Section Review

Metamorphic Rock

USING KEY TERMS

1. In your own words, define the following terms: *foliated* and *nonfoliated*.

UNDERSTANDING KEY IDEAS

_______ **2.** Which of the following is not a type of foliated metamorphic rock?

    a. gneiss

    b. slate

    c. marble

    d. schist

3. Explain the difference between contact metamorphism and regional metamorphism.

4. Explain how index minerals allow a scientist to understand the history of a metamorphic rock.

| Section Review *continued*

MATH SKILLS

5. For every 3.3 km a rock is buried, the pressure placed upon it increases 0.1 gigapascal (100 million pascals). If rock undergoing metamorphosis is buried at 16 km, what is the pressure placed on that rock? Show your work below.

CRITICAL THINKING

6. Making Inferences If you had two metamorphic rocks, one that has garnet crystals and the other that has chlorite crystals, which one could have formed at a deeper level in the Earth's crust? Explain your answer.

____

____

____

____

7. Applying Concepts Which do you think would be easier to break, a foliated rock, such as slate, or a nonfoliated rock, such as quartzite? Explain.

____

____

____

____

8. Analyzing Processes A mountain range is located at a boundary where two tectonic plates are colliding. Would most of the metamorphic rock in the mountain range be a product of contact metamorphism or regional metamorphism? Explain.

____

____

____

____

Chapter Review

USING KEY TERMS

1. In your own words, write a definition for the term *rock cycle*.

____

____

Complete each of the following sentences by choosing the correct term from the word bank.

stratification	foliated
extrusive igneous rock	texture

2. The _______________________ of a rock is determined by the sizes, shapes, and positions of the minerals the rock contains.

3. _______________________ metamorphic rock contains minerals that are arranged in plates or bands.

4. The most characteristic property of sedimentary rock is _______________________.

5. _______________________ forms plains called *lava plateaus*.

UNDERSTANDING KEY IDEAS

Multiple Choice

______ **6.** Sedimentary rock is classified into all of the following main categories except
  a. clastic sedimentary rock.
  b. chemical sedimentary rock.
  c. nonfoliated sedimentary rock.
  d. organic sedimentary rock.

______ **7.** An igneous rock that cools very slowly has a ______ texture.
  a. foliated
  b. fine-grained
  c. nonfoliated
  d. coarse-grained

Chapter Review *continued*

_______ **8.** Igneous rock forms when
    a. minerals crystallize from a solution.
    b. sand grains are cemented together.
    c. magma cools and solidifies.
    d. mineral grains in a rock recrystallize.

_______ **9.** A _____ is a common structure found in metamorphic rock.
    a. ripple mark   **c.** sill
    b. fold   **d.** layer

_______**10.** The process in which sediment is removed from its source and transported is called
    a. deposition.   **c.** weathering.
    b. erosion.   **d.** uplift.

_______**11.** Mafic rocks are
    a. light-colored rocks rich in calcium, iron, and magnesium.
    b. dark-colored rocks rich in aluminum, potassium, silica, and sodium.
    c. light-colored rocks rich in aluminum, potassium, silica, and sodium.
    d. dark-colored rocks rich in calcium, iron, and magnesium.

Short Answer

12. Explain how composition and texture are used by scientists to classify rocks.

____

____

13. Describe two ways a rock can undergo metamorphism.

____

____

14. Explain why some minerals only occur in metamorphic rocks.

____

____

15. Describe how each type of rock changes as it moves through the rock cycle.

____

____

16. Describe two ways rocks were used by early humans and ancient civilizations.

____

____

CRITICAL THINKING

17. Concept Mapping Use the following terms to construct a concept map: *rocks, metamorphic, sedimentary, igneous, foliated, nonfoliated, organic, clastic, chemical, intrusive,* and *extrusive.*

Chapter Review *continued*

18. Making Inferences If you were looking for fossils in the rocks around your home and the rock type that was closest to your home was metamorphic, do you think that you would find many fossils? Explain your answer.

____

____

____

____

19. Applying Concepts Imagine that you want to quarry, or mine, granite. You have all of the equipment, but you have two pieces of land to choose from. One area has a granite batholith underneath it. The other has a granite sill. If both intrusive bodies are at the same depth, which one would be the better choice for you to quarry? Explain your answer.

____

____

____

____

20. Applying Concepts The sedimentary rock coquina is made up of pieces of seashells. Which of the three kinds of sedimentary rock could coquina be? Explain your answer.

____

____

____

____

21. Analyzing Processes If a rock is buried deep inside the Earth, which geological processes cannot change the rock? Explain your answer.

____

____

____

INTERPRETING GRAPHICS

The bar graph below shows the percentage of minerals by mass that compose a sample of granite. Use the graph below to answer the questions that follow.

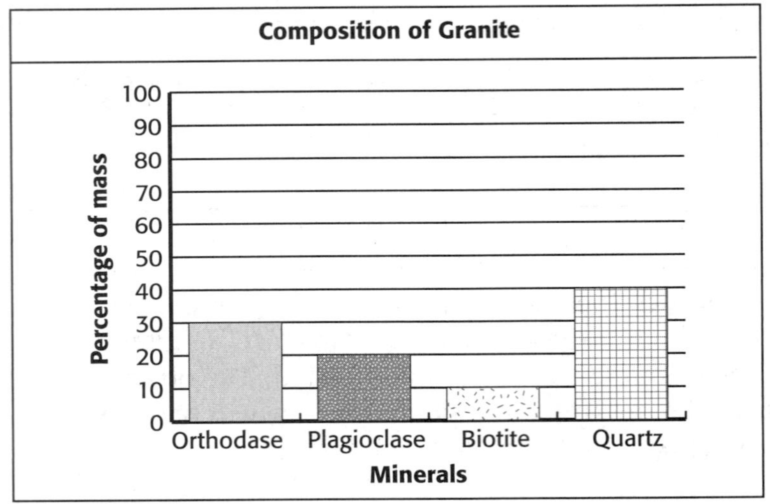

22. Your rock sample is made of four minerals. What percentage of each mineral makes up your sample?

____

23. Both plagioclase and orthoclase are feldspar minerals. What percentage of the minerals in your sample of granite are not feldspar minerals?

____

24. If your rock sample has a mass of 10 g, how many grams of quartz does it contain?

____

25. Use paper, a compass, and a protractor or a computer to make a pie chart. Show the percentage of each of the four minerals your sample of granite contains. (Look in the Appendix of this book for help on making a pie chart.)

____

____

____

____

____

Reinforcement

What Is It?

Complete this worksheet after you finish reading the section "Metamorphic Rock."

In the boxes on the left, identify the rock being described as sedimentary, igneous, or metamorphic. Then in the boxes on the right, write the appropriate description in the blanks provided.

<table>
<tr><td>

1.

It can be distinguished by its layers.

It comes in three main categories, clastic, chemical, and organic.

Its origin is usually layers of sediment.

What is it?

____

</td><td>

2.

Fill in the blanks below with *clastic*, *chemical*, or *organic*.

_____________ rocks form the remains of organisms.

_____________ rocks form when rock or mineral fragments stick together.

_____________ rocks form from solutions of minerals and water.

</td></tr>
<tr><td>

3.

It is a result of change in the structure, texture, or composition of a rock.

It comes in two textures, foliated and nonfoliated.

Its origin is intense heat and pressure.

What is it?

____

</td><td>

4.

Fill in the blanks with *foliated* or *nonfoliated*.

In _________ rock, the mineral grains are aligned, but in _________ rock, they are not aligned.

</td></tr>
<tr><td>

5.
Write a riddle like those above for the third kind of rock.

____

____

____

____

____

</td><td>

6.
What kind of rocks form when magma cools beneath the Earth's surface?

____

What kind of rocks form when magma cools on the Earth's surface?

____

</td></tr>
</table>

Critical Thinking

Between a Rock and a Hard Place

From the desk of: Rob Dobbs

Dear Doug,

Well I've finally decided to open a jewelry store!

As you know, I've always been interested in precious stones and gems. I recently learned that many rare gems, such as rubies, are created in a laboratory environment. In fact, these synthetic gems are created by duplicating the effects of nature, but at a much faster rate. Artificial gems are usually not as valuable as naturally occurring gems, but they aren't considered fakes either.

Before I start selling synthetic gems, I'd like to know more about the formation of natural and synthetic rocks. Because you are a certified gemologist, I thought you could help by answering the attached questions.

Rob Dobbs

USEFUL TERMS

synthetic produced by artificial means, usually chemical or mechanical

Help Doug answer Rob's list of questions below:

COMPREHENDING IDEAS

1. Most gemstones are metamorphic minerals. What conditions would the laboratory need to duplicate to create synthetic gems?

____

____

____

MAKING INFERENCES

2. Could the same laboratory techniques used for making synthetic gems be used for making synthetic sedimentary rock? Explain your answer.

____

____

____

____

Critical Thinking *continued*

DETERMINING CAUSE AND EFFECT

3. Metamorphic rocks are formed at various depths in the Earth. Why would the depth at which a rock forms determine its type?

____

____

____

____

____

____

COMPREHENDING IDEAS

4. Explain why metamorphic rock will form neither synthetically nor naturally if the temperature is too high.

____

____

____

DEMONSTRATING REASONED JUDGMENT

5. Explain how a diamond in a jewelry store could contain the carbon from a prehistoric animal.

HELPFUL HINTS

Think about the rock cycle.

____

____

____

____

____

____

Section Quiz

Section: The Rock Cycle

Match the correct definition with the correct term. Write the letter in the space provided.

_______ **1.** solid mixture of one or more minerals and organic matter

_______ **2.** process by which new rock forms from old rock

_______ **3.** process by which sediment is removed from its source

_______ **4.** process by which sediment is dropped and comes to rest

_______ **5.** the chemical makeup of a rock

_______ **6.** size, shape, and position of grains that make up a rock

a. composition

b. rock

c. erosion

d. texture

e. rock cycle

f. deposition

Write the letter of the correct answer in the space provided.

_______ **7.** Which of the following rocks is not normally used as a construction material?
    a. marble   **c.** limestone
    b. halite   **d.** granite

_______ **8.** Which of the following processes changes rock on Earth's surface?
    a. metamorphism
    b. erosion
    c. compaction
    d. cementation

_______ **9.** When sedimentary rock is exposed to heat and pressure, what does it change into?
    a. magma   **c.** sedimentary rock
    b. igneous rock   **d.** metamorphic rock

_______ **10.** Scientists classify rocks
    a. by composition and texture.   **c.** by mass.
    b. by volume.   **d.** by color and size.

Section Quiz

Section: Igneous Rock

Write the letter of the correct answer in the space provided.

_______ **1.** Which of the following are ways magma is formed?
    a. by compaction and cementation
    b. by melting and cooling
    c. by changes in composition
    d. by weathering and erosion

_______ **2.** What kind of texture does igneous rock have when magma cools slowly?
    a. coarse-grained
    b. large-grained
    c. fine-grained
    d. medium-grained

_______ **3.** What kind of texture does igneous rock have when magma cools rapidly?
    a. coarse-grained
    b. medium-grained
    c. large-grained
    d. fine-grained

_______ **4.** What kind of rock is formed when magma intrudes into other rock?
    a. extrusive igneous rock
    b. metamorphic rock
    c. intrusive igneous rock
    d. organic sedimentary rock

_______ **5.** What kind of rock is formed from lava that cools on the Earth's surface?
    a. organic sedimentary rock
    b. metamorphic rock
    c. intrusive igneous rock
    d. extrusive igneous rock

Section Quiz

Section: Sedimentary Rock

Write the letter of the correct answer in the space provided.

______ **1.** Which process forms sediment?
   a. weathering
   b. cementation
   c. compaction
   d. deposition

______ **2.** What are strata?
   a. mineral fragments
   b. minerals crystallized out of solution
   c. layers in sedimentary rock
   d. fossils in sedimentary rock

______ **3.** What kind of sedimentary rock can be cemented together by calcite or quartz?
   a. organic
   b. stratified
   c. chemical
   d. clastic

______ **4.** What kind of sedimentary rock is made from dissolved minerals?
   a. organic
   b. chemical
   c. stratified
   d. clastic

______ **5.** What kind of sedimentary rock is made from fossils?
   a. organic
   b. stratified
   c. chemical
   d. clastic

______ **6.** What is the process called in which sedimentary rocks are arranged in layers?
   a. erosion
   b. extrusion
   c. weathering
   d. stratification

Section Quiz

Section: Metamorphic Rock

Match the correct description with the correct term. Write the letter in the space provided.

_______ **1.** process other than heat that causes metamorphism

_______ **2.** process in which crystals in minerals change in size or composition

_______ **3.** metamorphic rock in which mineral grains are NOT arranged in planes or bands

_______ **4.** a change in the shape of rock caused by force

_______ **5.** metamorphic rock in which mineral grains are arranged in bands

_______ **6.** result of large pieces of rock deep within the Earth's crust colliding

a. foliated

b. pressure

c. recrystallization

d. deformation

e. nonfoliated

f. regional metamorphism

Chapter Test A

Rocks: Mineral Mixtures

MULTIPLE CHOICE

Write the letter of the correct answer in the space provided.

_______ **1.** How did humans use rocks in the past?
   a. to play sports
   b. to tell time
   c. to write
   d. to make tools

_______ **2.** Which of the following does NOT cause magma to form?
   a. an increase in pressure on rock
   b. a rise in temperature in rock
   c. a change in composition in rock
   d. a decrease in pressure on rock

_______ **3.** Sedimentary rock is formed through the process of
   a. cementation
   b. stratification.
   c. erosion.
   d. foliation.

_______ **4.** What has to increase for metamorphism to occur?
   a. weathering and erosion
   b. temperature and pressure
   c. melting and cooling
   d. compaction and cementation

_______ **5.** Besides weathering and erosion, what other forces shape the Earth's features?
   a. deposition and uplift
   b. exfoliation and foliation
   c. cementation and melting
   d. composition and texture

_______ **6.** When magma cools quickly, what kind of texture does rock have?
   a. coarse-grained
   b. large-grained
   c. medium-grained
   d. fine-grained

_______ **7.** What are the main categories of sedimentary rock?
    a. extrusive and intrusive
    b. clastic, chemical, and organic
    c. felsic and mafic
    d. foliated and nonfoliated

_______ **8.** When temperature and pressure change, what can happen to the minerals in rocks?
    a. They stay the same.
    b. They fragment and loosen.
    c. They bind closer together.
    d. They change into other minerals.

_______ **9.** During the rock cycle, what forms when magma cools?
    a. igneous rock
    b. sedimentary rock
    c. metamorphic rock
    d. foliated rock

_______ **10.** What do scientists call the rock that is formed when magma cools below the Earth's surface?
    a. extrusive igneous rock
    b. intrusive igneous rock
    c. eruptive rock
    d. volcanic rock

_______ **11.** Besides clastic and chemical, what is the other kind of sedimentary rock?
    a. extrusive
    b. foliated
    c. organic
    d. intrusive

_______ **12.** What kind of metamorphic rock has its mineral grains arranged in planes or bands?
    a. extrusive
    b. foliated
    c. nonfoliated
    d. intrusive

| Chapter Test A *continued*

_______**13.** Besides texture, how else are rocks classified?
  a. by the amount of foliation
  b. by their grain size
  c. by their grain shape
  d. by their composition

_______**14.** The process in which rocks change shape is called
  a. deformation.
  b. deposition.
  c. composition.
  d. foliation.

MATCHING

Match the correct definition with the correct term. Write the letter in the space provided.

_______**15.** naturally occurring solid mixture of one or more minerals and organic matter

_______**16.** process in which sediment is dropped and comes to rest

_______**17.** process by which new rock is made from old rock

_______**18.** the quality of a rock based on size and shape

_______**19.** process by which sediment is removed from its source

_______**20.** the chemical makeup of a rock

a. deposition

b. erosion

c. rock

d. texture

e. rock cycle

f. composition

MATCHING

Match the correct definition with the correct term. Write the letter in the space provided.

_______**21.** metamorphic rock in which mineral grains are NOT arranged in bands

_______**22.** layers found in sedimentary rocks

_______**23.** rock that cools at the Earth's surface

_______**24.** process in which layers in sedimentary rock are formed

_______**25.** rock that cools below the Earth's surface

a. stratification

b. nonfoliated

c. extrusive igneous rock

d. strata

e. intrusive igneous rock

Chapter Test B

Rocks: Mineral Mixtures

USING KEY TERMS

Use the terms from the following list to complete the sentences below. Each term may be used only once. Some terms may not be used.

stratification	composition	rock cycle
rock	nonfoliated rock	erosion
gradient	strata	deposition

1. The process in which layers of sedimentary rock are formed is

called ____________________________.

2. A rock whose mineral grains are NOT formed in bands is

called ____________________________.

3. Grains of sand are washed into rivers and oceans through the process

of ____________________________.

4. The minerals found in a rock determine its ____________________________.

5. Rocks change their composition during the ____________________________.

UNDERSTANDING KEY IDEAS

Write the letter of the correct answer in the space provided.

______ **6.** The process in which sediment is dropped and comes to rest is called
   a. deposition.
   b. stratification.
   c. cementation.
   d. foliation.

______ **7.** Which of the following is a coarse-grained igneous rock?
   a. shale
   b. marble
   c. granite
   d. gneiss

______ **8.** Partially decomposed plant material forms
   a. chemical sedimentary rock.
   b. fossiliferous limestone.
   c. clastic sedimentary rock.
   d. coal.

_______ **9.** When shale is exposed to slight heat and pressure, what foliated metamorphic rock does it become?
    a. schist
    b. gneiss
    c. phyllite
    d. slate

10. How is clastic sedimentary rock different from chemical sedimentary rock?

____

____

____

11. Describe how contact metamorphism is different from regional metamorphism.

____

____

____

12. What will a nonfoliated rock look like under a microscope?

____

____

____

13. How does limestone form?

____

____

____

14. How do rocks recrystallize?

____

____

____

Chapter Test B *continued*

CRITICAL THINKING

15. Why is rock a good building material?

____

____

____

16. What does an extrusive rock formation tell about what is going on below the Earth's surface?

____

____

____

17. Why is sedimentary rock more common on Earth's surface than metamorphic rock or igneous rock?

____

____

____

____

| Chapter Test B *continued*

CONCEPT MAPPING

18. Complete the concept map below using the following terms:

conglomerate   igneous rock   dikes   texture
erode   sedimentary rock   composition.

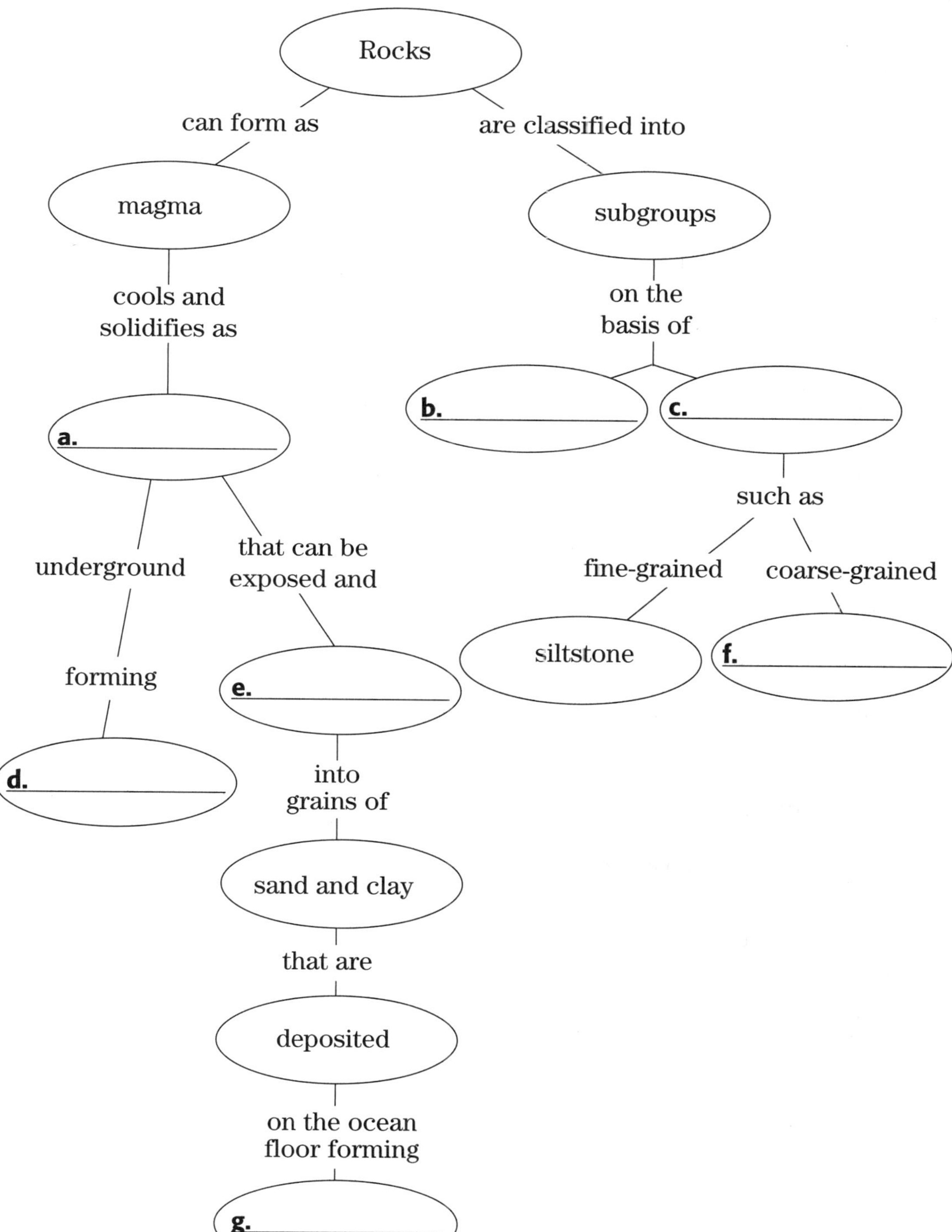

Chapter Test C

Rocks: Mineral Mixtures
MULTIPLE CHOICE

<u>Circle the letter</u> **of the best answer for each question.**

1. Which rock was used to construct the pyramids at Giza?

   a. granite

   b. marble

   c. slate

   d. limestone

2. What is the grain of igneous rock formed when magma cools quickly?

   a. fine-grained

   b. large-grained

   c. medium-grained

   d. coarse-grained

3. How does clastic sedimentary rock begin?

   a. as magma

   b. as plant remains

   c. as fragments of rock

   d. as animal remains

4. What do bends or folds in rocks show?

   a. They have been weathered.

   b. They have been deformed.

   c. They have cooled slowly.

   d. They have cooled rapidly.

Chapter Test C *continued*

MULTIPLE CHOICE

Circle the letter of the best answer for each question.

5. Besides being classified by their composition, how else are rocks classified?

  a. by their texture

  b. by their mass

  c. by their color

  d. by their volume

6. What occurs when temperature and pressure inside the Earth's crust change?

  a. stratification

  b. deformation

  c. deposition

  d. metamorphism

7. What is one way that magma forms?

  a. when rock is heated

  b. when rock is cooled

  c. when rock is cemented

  d. when rock is weathered

8. What are the layers of sedimentary rock called?

  a. sediment

  b. strata

  c. clasts

  d. folds

9. What is it called when sediment is dropped and comes to rest?

  a. erosion

  b. deposition

  c. weathering

  d. compaction

MATCHING

Read the description. Then, <u>draw a line</u> from the dot next to each description to the matching word.

10. the process by which new rock forms from old rocks ●

11. igneous rock that cools on the Earth's surface ●

12. rocks made from animal or plant remains ●

13. metamorphic rocks in which mineral grains are arranged in bands ●

a. organic sedimentary rock

b. extrusive igneous rock

c. foliated rock

d. rock cycle

| Chapter Test C *continued*

FILL-IN-THE-BLANK

Read the words in the box. Read the sentences. <u>Fill in each blank</u> with the word or phrase that best completes the sentence.

stratification	index minerals	intrusive igneous rock
uplift	erosion	

14. Weathering, erosion, deposition, and

________________________________ are the processes that shape the

Earth's surface.

15. The process in which sedimentary rocks are arranged in layers is

called ________________________________.

16. Minerals used to estimate temperature and pressure at which rock

changes are called ________________________________.

17. On the Earth's surface, weathering and

________________________________ make rock fragments.

18. Rock formed from magma that cools below the earth's surface is

________________________________.

 SKILLS PRACTICE

Performance-Based Assessment

OBJECTIVE

You will model the rock cycle to get a better understanding of the processes involved in changing rock from one phase to another.

KNOW THE SCORE!

As you work through the activity, keep in mind that you will be earning a grade for the following:

- how you work with the materials and equipment (30%)
- the quality of your observations (40%)
- your analysis of your observations (30%)

SAFETY INFORMATION 

- Never work with electricity near water. Also make sure the floor and all your work surfaces are dry.
- When using a hot plate, make sure you are wearing heat-resistant gloves, goggles, and an apron.
- Tie back your hair and make sure your clothing is not loose. Remove any jewelry you might be wearing.

MATERIALS

- 4 sugar cubes
- 2.5 mL (1/2 tsp) of vegetable oil
- 2.5 mL spoon
- 250 mL beaker
- craft stick
- heat-resistant gloves
- goggles
- hot plate
- long-handled spoon

PROCEDURE

1. Place four sugar cubes and 2.5 mL of vegetable oil in a beaker.
2. Wearing heat-resistant gloves and goggles, plug in the hot plate and turn it on. Place the beaker on the hot plate.
3. Stir the mixture with a craft stick until the sugar liquefies. Stir vigorously to prevent the sugar from turning brown and caramelizing.
4. Carefully remove the beaker from the hot plate. Turn off the hot plate. Allow the mixture to cool for at least 10 minutes. Do not touch the mixture until instructed to do so.
5. Carefully lift the cooled sugar from the beaker with a spoon. Wet your hands, and carefully tug and press the sugar mold.

Performance-Based Assessment *continued*

ANALYSIS

6. If sugar granules represent sediment eroded from other rock, what would each sugar cube represent? Explain your answer.

____

____

____

____

7. If sugar represents sedimentary rock, what did the sugar represent as it melted? Explain your answer.

____

____

____

8. If sugar represents sedimentary rock, what did it represent as it cooled after it melted? Explain your answer.

____

____

____

9. What type of rock is represented when the sugar was pressed after it cooled? Explain using the terms metamorphic and igneous.

____

____

10. Summarize the rock cycle by filling in the blanks below with the rock types modeled in this activity.

_________   _________   _________   _________

    was   was   was

    heated   cooled   pressed

    to form   to form   to form

Standardized Test Preparation

READING

Read each of the passages below. Then, answer the questions that follow each passage.

Passage 1 The texture and composition of a rock can provide good clues about how and where the rock formed. Scientists use both texture and composition to understand the <u>origin</u> and history of rocks. For example, marble is a rock that is made when limestone is metamorphosed. Only limestone contains the mineral—calcite—that can change into marble. Therefore, wherever scientists find marble, they know the sediment that created the original limestone was deposited in a warm ocean or lake environment.

_______ **1.** In the passage, what does the word *origin* mean?
   A size or appearance
   B age
   C location or surroundings
   D source or formation

_______ **2.** Based on the passage, what can the reader conclude?
   F Marble is a sedimentary rock.
   G Limestone is created by sediments deposited in warm ocean or lake environments.
   H Marble is a rock that is made when sandstone has undergone metamorphism.
   I In identifying a rock, the texture of a rock is more important than the composition of the rock.

_______ **3.** What is the main idea of the passage?
   A Scientists believe marble is the most important rock type to study.
   B Scientists study the composition and texture of a rock to determine how the rock formed and what happened after it formed.
   C Some sediments are deposited in warm oceans and lakes.
   D When limestone undergoes metamorphism, it creates marble.

Standardized Test Preparation *continued*

Passage 2 Fulgurites are a rare type of natural glass found in areas that have quartz-rich sediments, such as beaches and deserts. A <u>tubular</u> fulgurite forms when a lightning bolt strikes material such as sand and melts the quartz into a liquid. The liquid quartz cools and solidifies quickly, and a thin, glassy tube is left behind. Fulgurites usually have a rough outer surface and a smooth inner surface. Underground, a fulgurite may be shaped like the roots of a tree. The fulgurite branches out with many arms that trace the zigzag path of the lightning bolt. Some fulgurites are as short as your little finger, but others stretch 20 m into the ground.

______ **1.** In the passage, what does the word *tubular* mean?
   A flat and sharp
   B round and long
   C funnel shaped
   D pyramid shaped

______ **2.** From the information in the passage, what can the reader conclude?
   F Fulgurites are formed above ground.
   G Sand contains a large amount of quartz.
   H Fulgurites are most often very small.
   I Fulgurites are easy to find in sandy places.

______ **3.** Which of the following statements best describes a fulgurite?
   A Fulgurites are frozen lightning bolts.
   B Fulgurites are rootlike rocks.
   C Fulgurites are glassy tubes found in deserts.
   D Fulgurites are natural glass tubes formed by lightning bolts.

Standardized Test Preparation *continued*

INTERPRETING GRAPHICS

Use the diagram below to answer the questions that follow

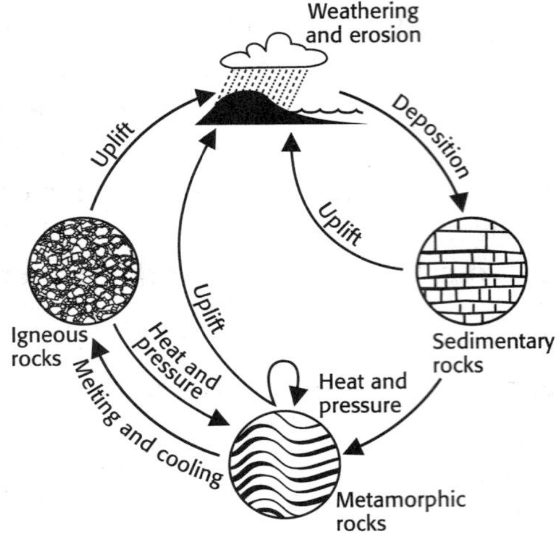

_______ **1.** According to the rock cycle diagram, which of the following
statements is true?
  A Only sedimentary rock gets weathered and eroded.
  B Sedimentary rocks are made from metamorphic, igneous, and
  sedimentary rock fragments and minerals.
  C Heat and pressure create igneous rocks.
  D Metamorphic rocks are created by melting and cooling.

_______ **2.** A rock exists at the surface of the Earth. What would be the next step
in the rock cycle?
  F cooling
  G weathering
  H melting
  I metamorphism

_______ **3.** Which of the following processes brings rocks to Earth's surface,
where they can be eroded?
  A burial
  B deposition
  C uplift
  D weathering

▌Standardized Test Preparation *continued*

Use the diagram on the previous page to answer the following question.

_______ **4.** Which of the following is the best summary of the rock cycle?

F Each type of rock gets melted. Then the magma turns into igneous, sedimentary, and metamorphic rock.

G Magma cools to form igneous rock. Then, the igneous rock becomes sedimentary rock. Sedimentary rock is heated and forms metamorphic rock. Metamorphic rock melts to form magma.

H All three rock types weather to create sedimentary rock. All three rock types melt to form magma. Magma forms igneous rock. All three types of rock form metamorphic rock because of heat and pressure.

I Igneous rock is weathered to create sedimentary rock. Sedimentary rock is melted to form igneous rock. Metamorphic rock is weathered to form igneous rock.

MATH

Read each question below and choose the best answer

_______ **1.** Eric has 25 rocks he has collected as a science project for class. Nine rocks are sedimentary, 10 are igneous, and 6 are metamorphic. If Eric chooses a rock at random, what is the probability that he will choose an igneous rock?

A 1/2

B 2/5

C 3/8

D 1/15

_______ **2.** At a mineral and fossil show, Elizabeth bought two quartz crystals that cost $2.00 each and four trilobite fossils that cost $3.50 each. Which equation can be used to describe c, the total cost of her purchase?

F $c = (2 \times 4) + (2.00 \times 3.50)$

G $c = (2 \times 2.00) + (4 \times 3.50)$

H $c = (4 \times 2.00) + (2 \times 3.50)$

I $c = (2 \times 2.00) + (4 + 3.50)$

Skills Practice Lab

DATASHEET FOR CHAPTER LAB

Let's Get Sedimental

How do we determine if sedimentary rock layers are undisturbed? The best way to do this is to be sure that fine-grained sediments near the top of a layer lie above coarse-grained sediments near the bottom of the layer. This lab activity will show you how to read rock features that will help you distinguish individual sedimentary rock layers. Then, you can look for the features in real rock layers.

OBJECTIVES

Model the process of sedimentation.

Determine whether sedimentary rock layers are undisturbed.

MATERIALS

- clay
- dropper pipet
- gravel
- magnifying lens
- mixing bowl, 2 qt
- soda bottle with a cap, plastic, 2 L
- sand
- scissors
- soil, clay rich, if available
- water

SAFETY 

PROCEDURE

1. In a mixing bowl, thoroughly mix the sand, gravel, and soil. Fill the soda bottle about one-third full of the mixture.

2. Add water to the soda bottle until the bottle is two-thirds full. Twist the cap back onto the bottle, and shake the bottle vigorously until all of the sediment is mixed in the rapidly moving water.

3. Place the bottle on a tabletop. Using the scissors, carefully cut the top off the bottle a few centimeters above the water, as shown. The open bottle will allow water to evaporate.

4. Immediately after you set the bottle on the tabletop, describe what you see from above and through the sides of the bottle.

____

____

5. Do not disturb the container. Allow the water to evaporate. (You may speed up the process by carefully using the dropper pipet to siphon off some of the clear water after you allow the container to sit for at least 24 hours.) You may also set the bottle in the sun or under a desk lamp to speed up evaporation.

6. After the sediment has dried and hardened, describe its surface.

____

____

7. Carefully lay the container on its side, and cut a wide, vertical strip of plastic down the length of the bottle to expose the sediments in the container. You may find it easier if you place pieces of clay on either side of the container to stabilize it. (If the bottle is clear along its length, this step may not be required.)

8. Brush away the loose material from the sediment, and gently blow on the surface until it is clean. Examine the surface, and record your observations.

____

____

ANALYZE THE RESULTS

1. Identifying Patterns Do you see anything through the side of the bottle that could help you determine if a sedimentary rock is undisturbed? Explain your answer.

____

____

____

____

2. Identifying Patterns Can you observe a pattern of deposition? If so, describe the pattern of deposition of sediment that you observe from top to bottom.

____

____

3. Explaining Events Explain how these features might be used to identify the top of a sedimentary layer in real rock and to decide if the layer has been disturbed.

____

____

____

____

Let's Get Sedimental *continued*

4. Identifying Patterns Do you see any structures through the side of the bottle that might indicate which direction is up, such as a change in particle density or size?

____

____

5. Identifying Patterns Use the magnifying lens to examine the boundaries between the gravel, sand, and silt. Do the size of the particles and the type of sediment change dramatically in each layer?

____

____

____

DRAW CONCLUSIONS

6. Making Predictions Imagine that a layer was deposited directly above the sediment in your bottle. Describe the composition of this new layer. Will it have the same composition as the mixture in steps 1–5 in the Procedure?

____

____

____

APPLYING YOUR DATA

With your class or with a parent, visit an outcrop of sedimentary rock. Apply the information that you have learned in this lab to see if you can determine whether the sedimentary rock layers are disturbed or undisturbed.

(Quick Lab)
Stretching Out

MATERIALS

- black ink pen
- paper
- plastic play putty

SAFETY INFORMATION 

PROCEDURE

1. Sketch the crystals in granite rock on a **piece of paper** with a **black-ink pen**. Be sure to include the outline of the rock, and fill it in with different crystal shapes.

2. Flatten some **plastic play putty** over your drawing, and slowly peel it off.

3. After making sure that the outline of your granite has been transferred to the putty, squeeze and stretch on the putty. What happened to the crystals in the granite? What happened to the granite?

____

____

Skills Practice Lab

Crystal Growth

DATASHEET FOR LABBOOK

Magma forms deep below the Earth's surface at depths of 25 km to 160 km and at extremely high temperatures. Some magma reaches the surface and cools quickly. Other magma gets trapped in cracks or magma chambers beneath the surface and cools very slowly. When magma cools slowly, large, well-developed crystals form. But when magma erupts onto the surface, it cools more quickly. There is not enough time for large crystals to grow. The size of the crystals found in igneous rocks gives geologists clues about where and how the rocks formed.

In this experiment, you will demonstrate how the rate of cooling affects the size of crystals in igneous rocks by cooling crystals of magnesium sulfate at two different rates.

Using Scientific Methods

MATERIALS

- aluminum foil
- basalt
- beaker, 400 mL
- gloves, heat-resistant
- granite
- hot plate
- laboratory scoop, pointed
- magnesium sulfate ($MgSO_4$) (Epsom salts)
- magnifying lens
- marker, dark
- pumice
- tape, masking
- test tube, medium-sized
- thermometer, Celsius
- tongs, test-tube
- watch (or clock)
- water, distilled
- water, tap, 200 mL

SAFETY INFORMATION 

ASK A QUESTION

1. How does temperature affect the formation of crystals?

FORM A HYPOTHESIS

2. Suppose you have two solutions that are identical in every way except for temperature. How will the temperature of a solution affect the size of the crystals and the rate at which they form?

____

____

Crystal Growth *continued*

TEST THE HYPOTHESIS

3. Put on your gloves, apron, and goggles.

4. Fill the beaker halfway with tap water. Place the beaker on the hot plate, and let it begin to warm. The temperature of the water should be between 40°C and 50°C. Caution: Make sure the hot plate is away from the edge of the lab table.

5. Examine two or three crystals of the magnesium sulfate with your magnifying lens. On a separate sheet of paper, describe the color, shape, luster, and other interesting features of the crystals.

6. On a separate sheet of paper, draw a sketch of the magnesium sulfate crystals.

7. Use the pointed laboratory scoop to fill the test tube about halfway with the magnesium sulfate. Add an equal amount of distilled water.

8. Hold the test tube in one hand, and use one finger from your other hand to tap the test tube gently. Observe the solution mixing as you continue to tap the test tube.

9. Place the test tube in the beaker of hot water, and heat it for approximately 3 min. Caution: Be sure to direct the opening of the test tube away from you and other students.

10. While the test tube is heating, shape your aluminum foil into two small boat-like containers by doubling the foil and turning up each edge.

11. If all the magnesium sulfate is not dissolved after 3 min, tap the test tube again, and heat it for 3 min longer. Caution: Use the test-tube tongs to handle the hot test tube.

12. With a marker and a piece of masking tape, label one of your aluminum boats "Sample 1," and place it on the hot plate. Turn the hot plate off.

13. Label the other aluminum boat "Sample 2," and place it on the lab table.

14. Using the test-tube tongs, remove the test tube from the beaker of water, and evenly distribute the contents to each of your foil boats. Carefully pour the hot water in the beaker down the drain. Do not move or disturb either of your foil boats.

15. Copy the table below onto a separate sheet of paper. Using the magnifying lens, carefully observe the foil boats. Record the time it takes for the first crystals to appear.

Crystal-Formation Table			
Crystal formation	**Time**	**Size and appearance of crystals**	**Sketch of crystals**
Sample 1			
Sample 2			

Crystal Growth *continued*

16. If crystals have not formed in the boats before class is over, carefully place the boats in a safe place. You may then record the time in days instead of in minutes.

17. When crystals have formed in both boats, use your magnifying lens to examine the crystals carefully.

ANALYZE THE RESULTS

1. Was your prediction correct? Explain.

____

____

____

____

2. Compare the size and shape of the crystals in Samples 1 and 2 with the size and shape of the crystals you examined in step 5. How long do you think the formation of the original crystals must have taken?

____

____

DRAW CONCLUSIONS

3. Granite, basalt, and pumice are all igneous rocks. The most distinctive feature of each is the size of its crystals. Different igneous rocks form when magma cools at different rates. Examine a sample of each with your magnifying lens.

4. Fill the table on the next page and sketch each rock sample.

Crystal Growth *continued*

5. Use what you have learned in this activity to explain how each rock sample formed and how long it took for the crystals to form. Record your answers in your table.

	Granite	Basalt	Pumice
How did the rock sample form?			
Rate of cooling			

COMMUNICATING YOUR DATA

Describe the size and shape of the crystals you would expect to find when a volcano erupts and sends material into the air and when magma oozes down the volcano's slope.

____

____

____

____

____

____

____

Metamorphic Mash

Metamorphism is a complex process that takes place deep within the Earth, where the temperature and pressure would turn a human into a crispy pancake. The effects of this extreme temperature and pressure are obvious in some metamorphic rocks. One of these effects is the reorganization of mineral grains within the rock. In this activity, you will investigate the process of metamorphism without being charred, flattened, or buried.

MATERIALS

- cardboard (or plywood), very stiff, small pieces
- clay, modeling
- knife, plastic
- sequins (or other small flat objects)

SAFETY INFORMATION 

PROCEDURE

1. Flatten the clay into a layer about 1 cm thick. Sprinkle the surface with sequins.
2. Roll the corners of the clay toward the middle to form a neat ball.
3. Carefully use the plastic knife to cut the ball in half. Describe the position and location of the sequins inside the ball.

____

____

4. Put the ball back together, and use the sheets of cardboard or plywood to flatten the ball until it is about 2 cm thick.
5. Using the plastic knife, slice open the slab of clay in several places. Describe the position and location of the sequins in the slab.

____

ANALYZE THE RESULTS

1. What physical process does flattening the ball represent?

____

____

____

Metamorphic Mash *continued*

2. Describe any changes in the position and location of the sequins that occurred as the clay ball was flattened into a slab.

____

____

DRAW CONCLUSIONS

3. How are the sequins oriented in relation to the force you put on the ball to flatten it?

____

____

4. Do you think the orientation of the mineral grains in a foliated metamorphic rock tells you anything about the rock? Defend your answer.

____

____

APPLYING YOUR DATA

Suppose you find a foliated metamorphic rock that has grains running in two distinct directions. Use what you have learned in this activity to offer a possible explanation for this observation.

____

____

____

____

Vocabulary Activity

Rockin' Connect Four

After you finishing reading the chapter, give this game a try! This game is for two people, X and O.

Rules

1. Choose who goes first.

2. Pick a square, and find the definition in the list below that matches the word in the square. Write the letter of the definition on the blank provided.

3. If the definition is correct, mark the square with your letter (X or O).

4. Your opponent chooses another square and finds the definition.

5. Continue playing until one player has four X's or four O's in a row horizontally, vertically, or diagonally.

DEFINITIONS

A. the makeup of a rock, usually according to the minerals present in it

B. igneous rock that forms when lava cools and solidifies on the Earth's surface

C. the texture of metamorphic rock in which mineral grains are aligned

D. rock that forms when magma or lava cools and solidifies

E. igneous rock that forms when magma cools and solidifies beneath the Earth's surface

F. a solid mixture of crystals of one or more minerals

G. hot liquid that forms when rock partially or completely melts

H. rock that forms when the texture and composition of a preexisting rock changes due to heat or pressure

I. the texture of metamorphic rock in which mineral grains show no alignment

J. the process by which one rock type changes into another rock type

K. rock that forms when sediments are pressed and cemented together

L. the layering of sedimentary rock

M. the sizes, shapes, and arrangement of grains that make up a rock

N. hot liquid that erupts onto the Earth's surface

O. long cracks in the Earth's surface

P. the layers of sedimentary rock

Vocabulary Activity *continued*

1. Rock cycle	**2.** Extrusive rock	**3.** Magma	**4.** Fissures
5. Composition	**6.** Igneous rock	**7.** Sedimentary rock	**8.** Nonfoliated
9. Intrusive rock	**10.** Stratification	**11.** Texture	**12.** Rock
13. Foliated	**14.** Lava	**15.** Metamorphic rock	**16.** Strata

SciLinks Activity

THE ROCK CYCLE

Go to www.scilinks.org. To find links related to the rock cycle, type in the keyword HSM0327. Then, use the links to create a story about the changes a piece of rock will undergo over time.

Imagine that you are a piece of igneous rock. You are looking forward to all the adventures (changes) that lie ahead of you. Use the space below to write a story about the cycle you will go through in the course of these changes. End your story when you are again a piece of igneous rock.

____

____

____

____

____

____

____

____

____

____

____

____

____

____

____

____

Performance-Based Assessment

Teacher Notes and Answer Key

PURPOSE

Students model the rock cycle to reinforce understanding
of the processes involved in changing rock from one phase
to another.

Yvonne Brannum
Hines Junior High
Washington, D.C.

TIME REQUIRED

One 45-minute class period.

Students will need 35 minutes at the activity station and 10 minutes to answer
the analysis questions.

RATING

Easy ←———1———2———3———4———→ Hard

Teacher Prep–1
Student Set-Up–2
Concept Level–2
Clean Up–1

ADVANCE PREPARATION

Equip each activity station with the necessary materials.

SAFETY INFORMATION

Caution students not to touch the sugar solution until you instruct them to do so.
Never work with electricity near water; be sure the floor and all work surfaces
are dry. Students should not heat glassware that is broken, chipped, or cracked.
They should use tongs or heatproof gloves to handle heated glassware. Students
should always wear heat-resistant gloves, goggles, and an apron when using a hot
plate. Never leave a hot plate unattended while it is turned on. Allow all equip
ment to cool before storing it. Students should tie back hair, secure clothing, and
remove loose jewelry.

TEACHING STRATEGIES

This activity works best in groups of 3–4 students. Conduct this activity after
covering "The Rock Cycle" in the chapter, "Rocks: Mineral Mixtures." Before the
activity, review the processes that cause one type of rock to change into another
and the characteristics that identify a rock as sedimentary, igneous, or
metamorphic.

If the sugar begins to caramelize at the beaker's base, it may produce smoke.
While students are waiting for the sugar mold to cool, they can work on the
analysis portion of the activity. After 10 minutes have passed, test the sugar mold
with wet hands before instructing students to handle it. The mold should be
warm but not hot. Remind students to wet their hands before stretching, pulling,
and pressing the sugar mold (taffy).

Performance-Based Assessment *continued*

Evaluation Strategies

Use the following rubric to help evaluate student performance

Rubric for Assessment

Possible points	Material and equipment use (30 points possible)
30–20	Successful completion of activity; safe and careful handling of materials and equipment; attention to detail; superior lab skills
19–10	Activity is generally complete; successful use of materials and equipment; sound knowledge of lab techniques; somewhat unfocused performance; mild neglect of safety measures
9–1	Attempts to complete activity yield inadequate results; unsafe lab technique; apparent lack of skill
	Quality and clarity of observation (40 points possible)
40–27	Good observations stated clearly and accurately; high level of detail; correct usage of scientific terminology
26–14	Complete observations; moderate level of detail, but expressed in unclear manner; minor inaccuracies, errors, or inconsistencies
13–1	Erroneous, incomplete, or unclear observations; lack of accuracy and detail
	Analysis (30 points possible)
30–20	Clear, detailed explanation shows good ability to make connections between the sugar model and the rock cycle
19–10	Adequate ability to make connections between the sugar model and the rock cycle; minor difficulty in expression
9–1	Poor ability to make connections between the sugar model and the rock cycle; explanation unclear or not relevant to rock cycle; substantial factual errors

Name _______________________________ Class ______________ Date ____________

(Assessment) **SKILLS PRACTICE**

Performance-Based Assessment

OBJECTIVE

You will model the rock cycle to get a better understanding of the processes involved in changing rock from one phase to another.

KNOW THE SCORE!

As you work through the activity, keep in mind that you will be earning a grade for the following:

- how you work with the materials and equipment (30%)
- the quality of your observations (40%)
- your analysis of your observations (30%)

SAFETY INFORMATION    

- Never work with electricity near water. Also make sure the floor and all your work surfaces are dry.
- When using a hot plate, make sure you are wearing heat-resistant gloves, goggles, and an apron.
- Tie back your hair and make sure your clothing is not loose. Remove any jewelry you might be wearing.

MATERIALS

- 4 sugar cubes
- 2.5 mL (1/2 tsp) of vegetable oil
- 2.5 mL spoon
- 250 mL beaker
- craft stick
- heat-resistant gloves
- goggles
- hot plate
- long-handled spoon

PROCEDURE

1. Place four sugar cubes and 2.5 mL of vegetable oil in a beaker.
2. Wearing heat-resistant gloves and goggles, plug in the hot plate and turn it on. Place the beaker on the hot plate.
3. Stir the mixture with a craft stick until the sugar liquefies. Stir vigorously to prevent the sugar from turning brown and caramelizing.
4. Carefully remove the beaker from the hot plate. Turn off the hot plate. Allow the mixture to cool for at least 10 minutes. Do not touch the mixture until instructed to do so.
5. Carefully lift the cooled sugar from the beaker with a spoon. Wet your hands, and carefully tug and press the sugar mold.

Name _______________________________ Class _______________ Date _______________

Performance-Based Assessment *continued*

ANALYSIS

6. If sugar granules represent sediment eroded from other rock, what would each sugar cube represent? Explain your answer.

The granules in a sugar cube have been compacted so that they stick together. If sugar granules represent sediment eroded from other rock, a sugar cube would represent sedimentary rock. Sedimentary rock forms when sediments are compacted and stick together.

7. If sugar represents sedimentary rock, what did the sugar represent as it melted? Explain your answer.

If sugar represents sedimentary rock and heat was applied to melt the sugar, the melting sugar represented molten magma. When sedimentary rock is heated so that it melts, it becomes magma.

8. If sugar represents sedimentary rock, what did it represent as it cooled after it melted? Explain your answer.

After the sugar melted and cooled, its cooled, solidified form represented igneous rock. Sedimentary rock that is heated until it melts and then cools becomes igneous rock.

9. What type of rock is represented when the sugar was pressed after it cooled? Explain using the terms metamorphic and igneous.

After the sugar was pulled and cooled, it represented metamorphic rock. Metamorphic rock forms when pressure is applied to igneous rock.

10. Summarize the rock cycle by filling in the blanks below with the rock types modeled in this activity.

sedimentary rock	→	magma	→	igneous rock	→	metamorphic rock
	was heated to form		was cooled to form		was pressed to form	

DATASHEET FOR CHAPTER LAB

Let's Get Sedimental

Teacher Notes and Answer Key

TIME REQUIRED

Two 45-minute class periods

RATING

Easy ⟵ 1   2   3   4 ⟶ Hard

Teacher Prep–1
Student Set-Up–2
Concept Level–2
Clean Up–2

MATERIALS

The materials listed are enough for a group of 3 or 4 students. You may substitute smaller plastic bottles. The amount of sand, gravel, and soil depends on the size of the jar. Each group will need enough of these materials to fill the bottle two-thirds full with a mixture of sand, gravel, and soil.

SAFETY CAUTION

Students should be extremely careful when cutting the sides from the plastic bottles.

PREPARATION NOTES

If the students use larger plastic bottles, the sediment may take several days to dry completely. It may be a good idea to ask the students to follow steps 1–5 as an introduction to the chapter. The class can then finish the procedure when the sediment has dried.

Name _________________________________ Class _______________ Date ______________

Let's Get Sedimental

DATASHEET FOR CHAPTER LAB

How do we determine if sedimentary rock layers are undisturbed? The best way to do this is to be sure that fine-grained sediments near the top of a layer lie above coarse-grained sediments near the bottom of the layer. This lab activity will show you how to read rock features that will help you distinguish individual sedimentary rock layers. Then, you can look for the features in real rock layers.

OBJECTIVES

Model the process of sedimentation.

Determine whether sedimentary rock layers are undisturbed.

MATERIALS

- clay
- dropper pipet
- gravel
- magnifying lens
- mixing bowl, 2 qt
- soda bottle with a cap, plastic, 2 L
- sand
- scissors
- soil, clay rich, if available
- water

SAFETY 

PROCEDURE

1. In a mixing bowl, thoroughly mix the sand, gravel, and soil. Fill the soda bottle about one-third full of the mixture.

2. Add water to the soda bottle until the bottle is two-thirds full. Twist the cap back onto the bottle, and shake the bottle vigorously until all of the sediment is mixed in the rapidly moving water.

3. Place the bottle on a tabletop. Using the scissors, carefully cut the top off the bottle a few centimeters above the water, as shown. The open bottle will allow water to evaporate.

4. Immediately after you set the bottle on the tabletop, describe what you see from above and through the sides of the bottle.

____

____

5. Do not disturb the container. Allow the water to evaporate. (You may speed up the process by carefully using the dropper pipet to siphon off some of the clear water after you allow the container to sit for at least 24 hours.) You may also set the bottle in the sun or under a desk lamp to speed up evaporation.

Name _________________________________ Class ______________ Date ______________

Let's Get Sedimental *continued*

6. After the sediment has dried and hardened, describe its surface.

____

____

7. Carefully lay the container on its side, and cut a wide, vertical strip of plastic down the length of the bottle to expose the sediments in the container. You may find it easier if you place pieces of clay on either side of the container to stabilize it. (If the bottle is clear along its length, this step may not be required.)

8. Brush away the loose material from the sediment, and gently blow on the surface until it is clean. Examine the surface, and record your observations.

____

____

ANALYZE THE RESULTS

1. Identifying Patterns Do you see anything through the side of the bottle that could help you determine if a sedimentary rock is undisturbed? Explain your answer.

Answers may vary. Students should understand that the finest sediments

should be at the top. This sequence can indicate the top of a layer in a

sedimentary outcrop. If the layers are not in this order, the rock may have

been disturbed.

2. Identifying Patterns Can you observe a pattern of deposition? If so, describe the pattern of deposition of sediment that you observe from top to bottom.

Students should indicate that in the sorting process, gravel settled out first,

followed by sand and then soil.

3. Explaining Events Explain how these features might be used to identify the top of a sedimentary layer in real rock and to decide if the layer has been disturbed.

If features that geologists expect to find only in the top layer are found

elsewhere, this finding indicates that the column has been disturbed.

Geologists carefully study the layers for these features so that they can

determine the original order of the layers.

____

Name _________________________________ Class _______________ Date ____________

Let's Get Sedimental *continued*

4. **Identifying Patterns** Do you see any structures through the side of the bottle that might indicate which direction is up, such as a change in particle density or size?

   Each layer should show finer particles at the top. This pattern can be seen

   only from the side.

5. **Identifying Patterns** Use the magnifying lens to examine the boundaries between the gravel, sand, and silt. Do the size of the particles and the type of sediment change dramatically in each layer?

   Students should see the same grading effect at the boundaries. The changes

   within each layer will be gradual, but the changes between different layers in

   the "rock" column may be more dramatic.

DRAW CONCLUSIONS

6. **Making Predictions** Imagine that a layer was deposited directly above the sediment in your bottle. Describe the composition of this new layer. Will it have the same composition as the mixture in steps 1–5 in the Procedure?

   If sediment having the same particle sizes as the mixture in steps 1-5 is

   deposited on top of the sediment in the bottle, the new layer should have the

   same composition as the layer in the bottle.

APPLYING YOUR DATA

With your class or with a parent, visit an outcrop of sedimentary rock. Apply the information that you have learned in this lab to see if you can determine whether the sedimentary rock layers are disturbed or undisturbed.

Name _________________________________ Class _______________ Date _____________

Quick Lab

Stretching Out

MATERIALS

- black ink pen
- paper
- plastic play putty

SAFETY INFORMATION 

PROCEDURE

1. Sketch the crystals in granite rock on a **piece of paper** with a **black-ink pen**. Be sure to include the outline of the rock, and fill it in with different crystal shapes.

2. Flatten some **plastic play putty** over your drawing, and slowly peel it off.

3. After making sure that the outline of your granite has been transferred to the putty, squeeze and stretch on the putty. What happened to the crystals in the granite? What happened to the granite?

The "crystals" become stretched and deformed. The "granite" changed its

shape because of the force applied to it.

Skills Practice Lab

Crystal Growth

DATASHEET FOR LABBOOK

Gordon Zibelman
Drexel Hill Middle School
Drexel Hill, Pennsylvania

Teacher Notes and Answer Key

TIME REQUIRED
Two 45-minute class periods

LAB RATINGS
Teacher Prep–2
Student Set-Up–3
Concept Level–2
Clean Up–2

Easy  Hard

MATERIALS

The materials listed are enough for a group of 4–5 students working coopera-
tively. Using a higher proportion of magnesium sulfate crystals to water will take
significantly longer.

SAFETY CAUTION

Remind students to review all safety cautions and icons before beginning this lab
activity.

PREPARATION NOTES

Samples of igneous rocks may be obtained locally or through various science
supply catalogs.

LAB NOTES

Some volcanic rocks contain both large and small crystals. This is because the
magma cooled for a period of time before erupting. This period of time was long
enough for some minerals to crystallize but too short for other minerals to form.

Name _________________________________ Class _______________ Date _______________

Skills Practice Lab)   **DATASHEET FOR LABBOOK**

Crystal Growth

Magma forms deep below the Earth's surface at depths of 25 km to 160 km and at extremely high temperatures. Some magma reaches the surface and cools quickly. Other magma gets trapped in cracks or magma chambers beneath the surface and cools very slowly. When magma cools slowly, large, well-developed crystals form. But when magma erupts onto the surface, it cools more quickly. There is not enough time for large crystals to grow. The size of the crystals found in igneous rocks gives geologists clues about where and how the rocks formed.

In this experiment, you will demonstrate how the rate of cooling affects the size of crystals in igneous rocks by cooling crystals of magnesium sulfate at two different rates.

Using Scientific Methods

MATERIALS

- aluminum foil
- basalt
- beaker, 400 mL
- gloves, heat-resistant
- granite
- hot plate
- laboratory scoop, pointed
- magnesium sulfate ($MgSO_4$) (Epsom salts)
- magnifying lens
- marker, dark
- pumice
- tape, masking
- test tube, medium-sized
- thermometer, Celsius
- tongs, test-tube
- watch (or clock)
- water, distilled
- water, tap, 200 mL

SAFETY INFORMATION 

ASK A QUESTION

1. How does temperature affect the formation of crystals?

FORM A HYPOTHESIS

2. Suppose you have two solutions that are identical in every way except for temperature. How will the temperature of a solution affect the size of the crystals and the rate at which they form?

____

____

Name _________________________________ Class _______________ Date _____________

Crystal Growth *continued*

TEST THE HYPOTHESIS

3. Put on your gloves, apron, and goggles.

4. Fill the beaker halfway with tap water. Place the beaker on the hot plate, and let it begin to warm. The temperature of the water should be between 40°C and 50°C. Caution: Make sure the hot plate is away from the edge of the lab table.

5. Examine two or three crystals of the magnesium sulfate with your magnifying lens. On a separate sheet of paper, describe the color, shape, luster, and other interesting features of the crystals.

6. On a separate sheet of paper, draw a sketch of the magnesium sulfate crystals.

7. Use the pointed laboratory scoop to fill the test tube about halfway with the magnesium sulfate. Add an equal amount of distilled water.

8. Hold the test tube in one hand, and use one finger from your other hand to tap the test tube gently. Observe the solution mixing as you continue to tap the test tube.

9. Place the test tube in the beaker of hot water, and heat it for approximately 3 min. Caution: Be sure to direct the opening of the test tube away from you and other students.

10. While the test tube is heating, shape your aluminum foil into two small boat-like containers by doubling the foil and turning up each edge.

11. If all the magnesium sulfate is not dissolved after 3 min, tap the test tube again, and heat it for 3 min longer. Caution: Use the test-tube tongs to handle the hot test tube.

12. With a marker and a piece of masking tape, label one of your aluminum boats "Sample 1," and place it on the hot plate. Turn the hot plate off.

13. Label the other aluminum boat "Sample 2," and place it on the lab table.

14. Using the test-tube tongs, remove the test tube from the beaker of water, and evenly distribute the contents to each of your foil boats. Carefully pour the hot water in the beaker down the drain. Do not move or disturb either of your foil boats.

15. Copy the table below onto a separate sheet of paper. Using the magnifying lens, carefully observe the foil boats. Record the time it takes for the first crystals to appear.

Crystal-Formation Table			
Crystal formation	**Time**	**Size and appearance of crystals**	**Sketch of crystals**
Sample 1			
Sample 2			

Name _______________________________ Class _______________ Date _____________

Crystal Growth *continued*

16. If crystals have not formed in the boats before class is over, carefully place the boats in a safe place. You may then record the time in days instead of in minutes.

17. When crystals have formed in both boats, use your magnifying lens to examine the crystals carefully.

ANALYZE THE RESULTS

1. Was your prediction correct? Explain.

Answers will vary. A correct prediction would state that a cool solution will produce crystals more quickly than a warm solution. A correct prediction would also state that the crystals produced in a warm solution will be much larger than those produced in a cool solution.

2. Compare the size and shape of the crystals in Samples 1 and 2 with the size and shape of the crystals you examined in step 5. How long do you think the formation of the original crystals must have taken?

Because the original crystals were small, students may conclude that they formed quickly.

DRAW CONCLUSIONS

3. Granite, basalt, and pumice are all igneous rocks. The most distinctive feature of each is the size of its crystals. Different igneous rocks form when magma cools at different rates. Examine a sample of each with your magnifying lens.

4. Fill the table on the next page and sketch each rock sample.

Accept all reasonable sketches.

Name _______________________________ Class ______________ Date ______________

Crystal Growth *continued*

5. Use what you have learned in this activity to explain how each rock sample formed and how long it took for the crystals to form. Record your answers in your table.

	Granite	**Basalt**	**Pumice**
How did the rock sample form?	when magma cools slowly beneath the Earth's surface	when lava cools quickly on the Earth's surface	when magma is ejected from a volcano during a violent eruption
Rate of cooling	cools slowly; large crystals	cools quickly; small crystals	cools very quickly; very small or no crystals

COMMUNICATING YOUR DATA

Describe the size and shape of the crystals you would expect to find when a volcano erupts and sends material into the air and when magma oozes down the volcano's slope.

Volcanic rocks that form in the air as the result of a violent volcanic eruption

would cool quickly and have small crystals. Volcanic rocks that form from lava

oozing out of a volcano would cool more slowly and have larger crystals.

____

____

____

____

____

____

Model-Making Lab

Metamorphic Mash

DATASHEET FOR LABBOOK

Teacher Notes and Answer Key

TIME REQUIRED

One 45-minute class period

LAB RATINGS

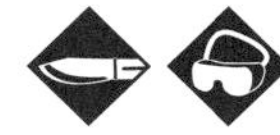

Teacher Prep–1
Student Set-Up–2
Concept Level–2
Clean Up–2

MATERIALS

The materials listed in the student page are enough for one student.

SAFETY CAUTION

Remind students to review all safety cautions and icons before beginning this lab activity.

Name _________________________________ Class _______________ Date ___________

Model-Making Lab) **DATASHEET FOR LABBOOK**

Metamorphic Mash

Metamorphism is a complex process that takes place deep within the Earth, where the temperature and pressure would turn a human into a crispy pancake. The effects of this extreme temperature and pressure are obvious in some metamorphic rocks. One of these effects is the reorganization of mineral grains within the rock. In this activity, you will investigate the process of metamorphism without being charred, flattened, or buried.

MATERIALS

- cardboard (or plywood), very stiff, small pieces
- clay, modeling
- knife, plastic
- sequins (or other small flat objects)

SAFETY INFORMATION 

PROCEDURE

1. Flatten the clay into a layer about 1 cm thick. Sprinkle the surface with sequins.

2. Roll the corners of the clay toward the middle to form a neat ball.

3. Carefully use the plastic knife to cut the ball in half. Describe the position and location of the sequins inside the ball.

The sequins should be lying in a random pattern. Any layering is the result

of rolling the ball.

4. Put the ball back together, and use the sheets of cardboard or plywood to flatten the ball until it is about 2 cm thick.

5. Using the plastic knife, slice open the slab of clay in several places. Describe the position and location of the sequins in the slab.

The sequins are all horizontal.

ANALYZE THE RESULTS

1. What physical process does flattening the ball represent?

It represents the pressure that creates metamorphic rock.

Name _______________________________ Class _______________ Date __________

Metamorphic Mash *continued*

2. Describe any changes in the position and location of the sequins that occurred as the clay ball was flattened into a slab.

Before the ball was flattened, the sequins were in a random pattern. Once

the ball was flattened, they lined up perpendicular to the pressure.

DRAW CONCLUSIONS

3. How are the sequins oriented in relation to the force you put on the ball to flatten it?

The sequins are aligned perpendicular to the force.

4. Do you think the orientation of the mineral grains in a foliated metamorphic rock tells you anything about the rock? Defend your answer.

Because the grains line up at right angles to the pressure, they are perpendi-

cular to the strongest stress.

APPLYING YOUR DATA

Suppose you find a foliated metamorphic rock that has grains running in two distinct directions. Use what you have learned in this activity to offer a possible explanation for this observation.

Answers will vary. Two pressures acting on the rock at different times must

have pushed on the rock in different directions.

Answer Key

Directed Reading A

SECTION: THE ROCK CYCLE

1. B
2. C
3. building materials
4. A
5. C
6. A
7. D
8. B
9. C
10. C
11. E
12. A
13. B
14. D
15. weathering
16. sediment
17. erosion
18. deposition
19. minerals
20. sedimentary
21. uplift
22. the Earth's surface
23. A
24. D
25. C
26. A
27. D
28. A
29. B

SECTION: IGNEOUS ROCK

1. B
2. A
3. the composition of the magma and the amount of time the magma takes to cool
4. magma
5. when rock is heated, when pressure is released, or when rock changes composition
6. temperature, pressure, and composition
7. Rather than solidifying at one exact temperature, magma cools at various temperatures, depending on its composition, because different minerals melt at different temperatures. Magma can be made up of various minerals in different mixtures. Some minerals within the magma will only solidify at low temperatures while other minerals will begin to solidify earlier when the temperature is still quite high.
8. dense
9. felsic rocks
10. mafic rocks
11. mineral crystals, coarse
12. finer
13. outside or slope
14. D
15. A
16. C
17. E
18. B
19. intrudes
20. coarse-grained
21. extrusive igneous rock
22. fissures
23. ocean floor
24. lava plateau

SECTION: SEDIMENTARY ROCK

1. sandstone
2. sedimentary rock
3. cement
4. surface
5. strata
6. clasts
7. clastic
8. texture
9. chemical
10. organic
11. coral, reefs
12. fossiliferous
13. coal
14. C
15. A
16. D
17. C

SECTION: METAMORPHIC ROCK

1. A
2. C
3. B
4. solid
5. mineral grains
6. contact metamorphism
7. distance, temperature
8. regional metamorphism
9. crust
10. B
11. C
12. D
13. C
14. A
15. D
16. F
17. C
18. A
19. E
20. B
21. D
22. A

Directed Reading B

SECTION: THE ROCK CYCLE

1. C
2. B
3. A
4. A
5. C
6. A
7. D
8. B
9. C
10. deposition
11. weathering
12. sediment
13. magma
14. C
15. A
16. D
17. A
18. B
19. D
20. A
21. D
22. B
23. D
24. A
25. B

SECTION: IGNEOUS ROCK

1. A
2. D
3. C
4. B
5. D
6. A
7. crystals
8. felsic rocks
9. mafic rocks
10. cooled
11. fine
12. A
13. D
14. B
15. C
16. D
17. A
18. B

SECTION: SEDIMENTARY ROCK

1. weather
2. sediment
3. erosion
4. sediment
5. dissolved minerals
6. strata
7. C
8. D
9. B
10. A
11. C
12. C
13. A
14. D
15. fossils
16. coral
17. reefs
18. fossiliferous limestone
19. coal
20. B
21. D
22. B

SECTION: METAMORPHIC ROCK

1. C
2. B
3. A
4. D
5. B
6. C
7. A
8. pressure

9. stable
10. index minerals
11. foliated
12. slate
13. phyllite
14. gneiss
15. C
16. B
17. D
18. D
19. B

Vocabulary and Section Summary

SECTION: THE ROCK CYCLE

1. rock cycle: continual process by which new rock forms from old rock
2. rock: naturally occurring solid mixture of one or more minerals and organic matter
3. erosion: the process by which sediment is removed from its source
4. deposition: the process by which material is laid down
5. composition: the minerals a rock contains
6. texture: the size, shape, and position of the grains that make up a rock

SECTION: IGNEOUS ROCK

1. intrusive igneous rock: rock that is formed when magma pushes into surrounding rock beneath the Earth's surface
2. extrusive igneous rock: rock that forms when magma erupts onto the Earth's surface

SECTION: SEDIMENTARY ROCK

1. strata: layers found in sedimentary rock
2. stratification: the process in which sedimentary rocks are arranged in layers

SECTION: METAMORPHIC ROCK

1. foliated: the texture of metamorphic rock in which the minerals are arranged in planes or bands
2. nonfoliated: the texture of metamorphic rock in which the mineral grains are not arranged in planes or bands

Section Review

SECTION: THE ROCK CYCLE

1. composition
2. Rock
3. B
4. Rock has been used by humans to make tools and weapons and to construct buildings.
5. Four processes that change rock inside the Earth are compaction and cementation, metamorphism, melting, and cooling.
6. Weathering is the process by which water, wind, ice, and heat break down rock. Erosion is the process by which sediment is removed from its source. Deposition is the process by which sediment moved by erosion is laid down. Uplift is the process by which rock within the Earth moves to Earth's surface.
7. Answers will vary. Sample answer: Fine grains in an igneous rock indicate that the rock cooled quickly, which means it was likely to have formed at Earth's surface.
8. Composition is the percent of elements that make up a rock. Texture is a quality of a rock that is based on the size, shape, and position of its grains.
9. Answers will vary. Sample answer: Rock is continually recycled by different processes in the rock cycle. Melting of sedimentary, metamorphic, or igneous rock creates new igneous rock. The weathering, erosion, deposition, burial, compression, and cementation of igneous, metamorphic, or sedimentary rock creates new sedimentary rock. Igneous, sedimentary, or metamorphic rock that is subjected to increased heat and pressure can be metamorphosed.
10. a medium-grained texture

SECTION: IGNEOUS ROCK

1. Answers will vary. Sample answer: Intrusive rock forms from magma that solidifies underground. Extrusive rock forms from magma that solidifies after it has reached the surface.
2. C

3. Temperature, pressure, and a change in the composition of a rock can cause magma to form. A rise in temperature can cause minerals in a rock to melt, forming magma. When pressure in a rock that is hot is released, the minerals in that rock can melt, forming magma. When fluids such as water combine with rock, the composition of the rock changes. This change in composition lowers the melting point of the rock enough to melt it, forming magma.

4. When magma cools slowly, crystals have a long time to grow, so the igneous rock that forms is coarse grained. When magma cools quickly, crystals have a short time to grow, so the igneous rock that forms is fine grained.

5. 1,825 ft $\div$ 3.28 m = 556.4 m

6. A sill intrudes rock parallel to the surrounding rock layers. A dike cuts across the surrounding rock layers.

7. Because the rock formed from slowly cooling magma deep inside the Earth, he crystals had more time to grow. Therefore, the texture of the rock would most likely be coarse-grained.

SECTION: SEDIMENTARY ROCK

1. Answers will vary. Sample answer: Strata are layers in sedimentary rock. Stratification is the process in which layers are arranged into sedimentary rock.

2. C

3. Clastic sedimentary rock is formed by the processes of weathering, erosion, deposition, compaction, and cementation. Rocks are physically weathered into fragments called sediment. Sediment is transported by erosion and is deposited in layers. Older layers of sediments are compacted by younger layers of sediments. Sediments in layers that have been compacted are cemented together by minerals that are dissolved in water, such as calcite and quartz, forming clastic sedimentary rock.

4. Clastic sedimentary rock forms when sediments are compacted and cemented together. Chemical sedimentary rock forms when dissolved minerals separate out of solution and crystallize. Organic sedimentary rock is made from the remains of animals that once lived in the ocean.

5. 2 m = 2,000 mm; 2,000 mm $\div$ 4 mm/yr = 500 yrs

6. Texture is more useful in classifying clastic sedimentary rock because the size of the grain can provide clues to where and how the rock was formed.

7. Answers will vary. Sample answer: The finer the grains of sediment are, the more likely delicate structures such as raindrop impressions will be preserved in them.

SECTION: METAMORPHIC ROCK

1. Answers will vary. Sample answer: Foliated metamorphic rock consists of minerals that are arranged in planes or bands. The minerals in nonfoliated metamorphic rock do not appear to be arranged in a pattern.

2. C

3. Contact metamorphism is a type of metamorphism that occurs near igneous intrusions, where magma comes into direct contact with surrounding rock. Regional metamorphism is a type of metamorphism that occurs when large pieces of Earth's crust collide, causing rock to become deformed and chemically changed over large areas.

4. Because index minerals form only at certain temperatures and pressures, index minerals indicate the temperature, pressure, and depth at which a rock metamorphosed

5. 16 km $\div$ 3.3 km = 4.84 km $\times$ 0.1 gigapascal = 0.484 gigapascal $+$ .101 gigapascal (atmospheric pressure) = .585 gigapascal

6. The rock with garnet crystals would probably have formed deeper in the Earth because the mineral garnet forms at a higher temperature and at a higher pressure than the mineral chlorite.

7. Because the grains in a foliated metamorphic rock are arranged in parallel bands, foliated metamorphic rock would be easier to break than a nonfoliated metamorphic rock.

8. Rock becomes deformed and chemically changed over large areas of Earth's crust by increases in temperature and pressure that occur when tectonic plates collide. Therefore, most of the rock in the mountain range would be the product of regional metamorphism.

Chapter Review

1. Answers will vary. Sample answer: The rock cycle is the process in which one rock type changes into another rock type. In this process, rock is continuously recycled.
2. texture
3. Foliated
4. stratification
5. Extrusive igneous rock
6. C
7. D
8. C
9. B
10. B
11. D
12. Scientists use differences in composition, or the minerals a rock is made up of, to classify rock. Scientists use differences in texture—the sizes, shapes, and positions of the grains a rock is made up of—to further classify rocks.
13. Two ways in which a rock can undergo metamorphism is by contact metamorphism and regional metamorphism. Contact metamorphism occurs near igneous intrusions, where magma comes in direct contact with the surrounding rock. Regional metamorphism occurs when pressure builds up in deep rock or when large pieces of earth's crust collide, deforming and chemically changing rock over large areas.
14. Some minerals can form only at specific pressures and temperatures present during metamorphism.

15. Answers will vary. Sample answer: When rocks are buried, they are heated and squeezed to create metamorphic rock. Sometimes the heat is enough to melt the rock and create magma, which cools to form igneous rock. Buried rocks are uplifted, and when rocks at the Earth's surface are eroded, sediments are created. These sediments later harden into sedimentary rock.
16. Two ways rock was used by early humans and ancient civilizations were as tools and as building materials.
17. An answer to this exercise can be found at the end of this book.
18. You would not find many—or any—fossils where you lived because fossils are usually found in sedimentary rock, not metamorphic rock. (Occasionally, fossils are preserved in metamorphic rock that was once sedimentary rock.)
19. The property with the batholith would be a better buy because batholiths are much bigger than sills.
20. The seashells that make up coquina are made up of the remains of once-living organisms, so coquina is an organic sedimentary rock. (The shells are technically clasts because they are particles that have been deposited.)
21. A rock buried deep beneath the surface cannot be changed by weathering and erosion, which are geological processes that change Earth's surface features.
22. orthoclase = 30 percent, plagioclase = 20 percent, biotite = 10 percent, quartz = 40 percent
23. plagioclase + orthoclase = 30% + 20% = 50%
100% − 50% = 50%
Fifty percent of the minerals in the granite are not feldspars.
24. 10 g × 0.40 = 4 g
25. Accept all reasonable responses. Charts should show the correct percentages of the minerals.

Reinforcement

WHAT IS IT?
1. a sedimentary rock
2. organic sedimentary, clastic sedimentary, and chemical sedimentary
3. a metamorphic rock
4. foliated, nonfoliated
5. Accept any reasonable answer. Sample answer: It is the result of the cooling of magma. It can be intrusive or extrusive. Its origin is magma. What is it? an igneous rock
6. intrusive igneous rocks, extrusive igneous rocks

Critical Thinking

BETWEEN A ROCK AND A HARD PLACE
1. Large amounts of heat and pressure would be necessary to form synthetic gemstones in a laboratory.
2. Heat and pressure would not make synthetic sedimentary rock because it is formed by the gradual accumulation of sediment, not by heat and pressure.
3. As the depth of the Earth increases, so does the amount of pressure. The composition of the surrounding rocks also changes as depth increases. Both composition and pressure determine the type of metamorphic rock that forms.
4. At temperatures greater than 1,000°C, rock usually melts into magma.
5. The carbon from a prehistoric animal could be preserved in sedimentary rock. As the Earth's crust moves, that rock is forced downward into the Earth. There the great temperature and pressure could transform elements of a sedimentary rock into a metamorphic mineral, such as a diamond.

Section Quizzes

SECTION: THE ROCK CYCLE
1. B
2. E
3. C
4. F
5. A
6. D
7. B
8. D
9. D
10. A

SECTION: IGNEOUS ROCK
1. C
2. A
3. D
4. C
5. D

SECTION: SEDIMENTARY ROCK
1. A
2. C
3. D
4. B
5. A
6. D

SECTION: METAMORPHIC ROCK
1. B
2. C
3. E
4. D
5. A
6. F

Chapter Test A
1. D
2. A
3. A
4. B
5. A
6. D
7. B
8. D
9. A
10. B
11. C
12. B
13. D
14. A
15. C
16. A
17. E
18. D
19. B
20. F
21. B
22. D
23. C
24. A

25. E

Chapter Test B

1. stratification
2. nonfoliated rock
3. erosion
4. composition
5. rock cycle
6. A
7. C
8. D
9. D
10. Answers will vary. Sample answer: Clastic sedimentary rock is formed from rock fragments that are cemented together by calcite or quartz. Chemical sedimentary rock is made of dissolved minerals that eventually crystallize.
11. Answers will vary. Sample answer: Contact metamorphism occurs when magma comes into direct contact with rock. Regional metamorphism occurs when large pieces of the Earth's crust collide with each other.
12. Answers will vary. Sample answer: Under a microscope a nonfoliated rock will not have mineral grains that are aligned.
13. Answers will vary. Sample answer: Limestone is formed from the remains, or fossils, of animals that once lived in the ocean.
14. Answers will vary. Sample answer: Rocks recrystallize when the crystals of the minerals change in composition.
15. Rocks like granite and marble are good building materials because they can withstand weathering for long periods of time.
16. Answers will vary. Sample answer: An extrusive rock formation reveals that there is a lot of activity, perhaps volcanic, going on below the Earth's surface.
17. All three rock types weather when they are uplifted to the earth's surface, forming sediments that cover the Earth's surface
18. **a.** igneous rock
    b. composition
    c. texture
    d. dikes
    e. erode
    f. conglomerate
    g. sedimentary rock

Chapter Test C

1. D
2. A
3. C
4. B
5. A
6. D
7. A
8. B
9. B
10. D
11. B
12. A
13. C
14. uplift
15. stratification
16. index minerals
17. erosion
18. intrusive igneous rock

Standardized Test Preparation

READING
Passage 1
1. D
2. G
3. B

Passage 2
1. B
2. G
3. D

INTERPRETING GRAPHICS
1. B
2. G
3. C
4. H

MATH
1. B
2. G

Vocabulary Activity

1. J	**9.** E
2. B	**10.** L
3. G	**11.** M
4. O	**12.** F
5. A	**13.** C
6. D	**14.** N
7. K	**15.** H
8. I	**16.** P

SciLinks Activity

Answers may vary, but should trace the cycle in a progression beginning with igneous rock to sedimentary rock to metamorphic rock to finally igneous rock.

Lesson Plan

Section: The Rock Cycle

Pacing

Regular Schedule: **with lab(s):** N/A   **without lab(s):** 1 day
Block Schedule: **with lab(s):** N/A   **without lab(s):** 0.5 day

Objectives

1. Describe two ways rocks have been used by humans.

2. Describe four processes that shape Earth's features.

3. Describe how each type of rock changes into another type as it moves through the rock cycle.

4. List two characteristics of rock that are used to help classify it.

National Science Education Standards Covered

SAI 1 Abilities necessary to do scientific inquiry

SAI 2 Understandings about scientific inquiry

UCP 1 Systems, order, and organization

ST 2 Understandings about science and technology

SPSP 5 Science and technology in society

HNS 1 Science as a human endeavor

ES 1d Some changes in the solid earth can be described as the "rock cycle." Old rocks at the earth's surface weather, forming sediments that are buried, then compacted, heated, and often recrystallized into new rock. Eventually, those new rocks may be brought to the surface by the forces that drive plate motions, and the rock cycle continues.

ES 2b Fossils provide important evidence of how life and environmental conditions have changed.

KEY
SE = Student Edition   **TE** = Teacher's Edition
CRF = Chapter Resource File

FOCUS (*5 minutes*)

- **Chapter Starter Transparency** Use this transparency to introduce the chapter.

- **Bellringer, TE** Have students speculate on the answers to questions about what it would take to recycle a rock.

- **Bellringer, Transparency** Use this transparency as students enter the classroom and find their seats.

MOTIVATE *(10 minutes)*

_ **Discussion, Geologic Time, TE** Discuss the geologic time scale with students to give them an idea of how long the Earth has existed. **(GENERAL)**

TEACH *(20 minutes)*

_ **Reading Strategy, SE** Have students make a flow chart of the steps of the rock cycle.

_ **Group Activity, Rates of Weathering, TE** Have students visit a cemetery and measure weathering rates of grave markers. **(GENERAL)**

_ **Cultural Awareness, Stone Cities, TE** Have students write a report about or build a model of an ancient walled city. **(GENERAL)**

_ **Inclusion Strategies, TE** Groups of students use different foods to model sedimentary, metamorphic, and igneous rocks and minerals.

_ **Connection to Math, Percentages, TE** Explain to students about how a percentage is a ratio expressed in hundredths and how it is used to analyze pure substances and their composition. **(GENERAL)**

_ **Group Activity, Describing Rocks, TE** Have groups use dental picks, mineral identification keys, and a magnifying glass to analyze different samples of rocks and then report their findings to the class. **(BASIC)**

_ **Directed Reading A/B, CRF** These worksheets reinforce basic concepts and vocabulary presented in the lesson. **(BASIC/SPECIAL NEEDS)**

_ **Vocabulary and Section Summary, CRF** Students write definitions of key terms and read a summary of section content. **(GENERAL)**

_ **SciLinks Activity, The Rock Cycle, SciLinks code HSM 0327, CRF** Students research Internet resources related to rock composition. **(GENERAL)**

_ **Teaching Transparency, The Rock Cycle** Use this graphic to discuss the rock cycle.

CLOSE *(10 minutes)*

_ **Reteaching, Diagramming the Rock Cycle, TE** Have students create a diagram of the processes that shape Earth's surface. **(GENERAL)**

_ **Quiz, TE** Students answer 3 questions about the rock cycle.

_ **Alternative Assessment, Rock Cycle Skit, TE** Have students write and perform a skit that portrays the rock cycle. **(GENERAL)**

_ **Homework, TE** Have students make a poster that illustrates the rock cycle. **(GENERAL)**

_ **Section Review, CRF** Students answer end-of-section vocabulary, key ideas, critical thinking, and interpreting graphics questions. **(GENERAL)**

_ **Section Quiz, CRF** Students answer 10 objective questions about the rock cycle. **(BASIC/SPECIAL NEEDS)**

Lesson Plan

Section: Igneous Rock

Pacing

Regular Schedule: **with lab(s):** N/A   **without lab(s):** 1 day

Block Schedule: **with lab(s):** N/A   **without lab(s):** 0.5 day

Objectives

1. Describe three ways that igneous rock forms.

2. Explain how the cooling rate of magma affects the texture of igneous rock.

3. Distinguish between igneous rock that cools within Earth's crust and igenous rock that cools at Earth's surface.

National Science Education Standards Covered

SAI 1 Abilities necessary to do scientific inquiry

SAI 2 Understandings about scientific inquiry

UCP 1 Systems, order, and organization

UCP 2 Evidence, models, and explanation

ES 1c Land forms are the result of a combination of constructive and destructive forces. Constructive forces include crystal deformation, volcanic eruption, and deposition of sediment, while destructive forces include weathering and erosion.

ES 1d Some changes in the solid earth can be described as the "rock cycle." Old rocks at the earth's surface weather, forming sediments that are buried, then compacted, heated, and often recrystallized into new rock. Eventually, those new rocks may be brought to the surface by the forces that drive plate motions, and the rock cycle continues.

KEY

SE = Student Edition   **TE** = Teacher's Edition

CRF = Chapter Resource File

FOCUS (*5 minutes*)

_ **Bellringer, TE** Ask students to speculate on whether rocks made from cooled lava inside the Earth would look different from those which have cooled from lava on the Earth's surface.

_ **Bellringer, Transparency** Use this transparency as students enter the classroom and find their seats.

MOTIVATE *(10 minutes)*

_ **Discussion, Volcanoes, TE** Ask students to discuss how volcanoes affect people while informing them that lava and magma form very fertile land. **(GENERAL)**

TEACH *(20 minutes)*

_ **Reading Strategy, SE** Have students construct a table that compares intrusive and extrusive igneous rock.

_ **Using the Figure, Making Inferences, TE** Have students rank rocks based on how quickly the rocks cooled. **(BASIC)**

_ **Connection to Life Science, Life Along a Rift, TE** Students research the life-forms found in and around black smokers. **(ADVANCED)**

_ **Vocabulary and Section Summary, CRF** Students write definitions of key terms and read a summary of section content. **(GENERAL)**

_ **Directed Reading, A/B, CRF** These worksheets reinforce basic concepts and vocabulary presented in the lesson. **(BASIC/SPECIAL NEEDS)**

CLOSE *(10 minutes)*

_ **Reteaching, Word Meanings, TE** Have students brainstorm the prefixes *in-* and *ex-* to help them remember the meaning of *extrusive* and *intrusive*. **(BASIC)**

_ **Quiz, TE** Students answer 2 questions about igneous rock.

_ **Alternative Assessment, Modeling Igneous Rock Bodies, TE** Students use colored modeling clay to create a cross section that shows the formation of intrusive and extrusive igneous rock. **(GENERAL)**

_ **Homework, Volcanic Necks, TE** Have students research a volcanic neck formation to learn how one is formed. **(ADVANCED)**

_ **Section Review, CRF** Students answer end-of-section vocabulary, key ideas, math, and critical thinking questions. **(GENERAL)**

_ **Section Quiz, CRF** Students answer 5 objective questions about igneous rock. **(GENERAL)**

Lesson Plan

Section: Sedimentary Rock

Pacing

Regular Schedule: **with lab(s):** 2 days   **without lab(s):** 1 day

Block Schedule: **with lab(s):** 1 day   **without lab(s):** 0.5 day

Objectives

1. Describe the origin of sedimentary rock.

2. Describe the three main categories of sedimentary rock.

3. Describe three types of sedimentary structures.

National Science Education Standards Covered

SAI 1 Abilities necessary to do scientific inquiry

SAI 2 Understandings about scientific inquiry

UCP 1 Systems, order, and organization

UCP 2 Evidence, models, and explanation

ES 1c Land forms are the result of a combination of constructive and destructive forces. Constructive forces include crustal deformation, volcanic eruption, and deposition of sediment, while destructive forces include weathering and erosion.

ES 1d Some changes in the solid earth can be described as the "rock cycle." Old rocks at the earth's surface weather, forming sediments that are buried, then compacted, heated, and often recrystallized into new rock. Eventually, those new rocks may be brought to the surface by the forces that drive plate motions, and the rock cycle continues.

ES 1k Living organisms have played many roles in the earth system, including affecting the composition of the atmosphere, producing some types of rocks, and contributing to the weathering of rocks.

ES 2b Fossils provide important evidence of how life and environmental conditions have changed.

KEY

SE = Student Edition   **TE** = Teacher's Edition

CRF = Chapter Resource File

FOCUS (*5 minutes*)

- **Bellringer, TE** Ask students to compare in writing how the rings in a tree are like the layers of sedimentary rock.

- **Bellringer, Transparency** Use this transparency as students enter the classroom and find their seats.

MOTIVATE *(10 minutes)*

_ **Demonstration, Dissolution of Minerals, TE** Show students that water contains dissolved minerals, and have them observe ice cubes melting in warm water. (**GENERAL**)

TEACH *(65 minutes)*

_ **Reading Strategy, SE** Have students make an outline of the section as they read using the headings as a guide.

_ **Activity, Sedimentary Rock, TE** Have different groups of students investigate and prepare a report on how sandstone, shale, and limestone form and their use by humans. (**BASIC**)

_ **Connection to Life Science, Calcium Carbonate Critters, TE** Have students research a fossil locality in their state to learn more about fossils. (**BASIC**)

_ **Connection Activity, Real World, Uses of Organic Sedimentary Rock, TE** Students research and report to the class on the different uses of organic sedimentary rock. (**GENERAL**)

_ **Vocabulary and Section Summary, CRF** Students write definitions of key terms and read a summary of section content. (**GENERAL**)

_ **Directed Reading, A/B, CRF** These worksheets reinforce basic concepts and vocabulary presented in the lesson. (**BASIC/SPECIAL NEEDS**)

_ **Chapter Lab, Let's Get Sedimental, SE** Students model the process of sedimentation and determine whether sedimentary rock layers are undisturbed. (**GENERAL**)

_ **Datasheet for Chapter Lab, Let's Get Sedimental, CRF** Students use the datasheet to complete the Chapter Lab. (**GENERAL**)

CLOSE *(10 minutes)*

_ **Reteaching, Creating a Diagram, TE** Students create a diagram that illustrates the processes involved in the formation of one of the three types of sedimentary rock. (**BASIC**)

_ **Quiz, TE** Students answer 2 questions about sedimentary rock.

_ **Alternative Assessment, Depositional Environments, TE** Have students draw two pictures: one to show where sediments come from and how they are deposited, and the other to show what happens after sediments have built up layers for millions of years. (**GENERAL**)

_ **Section Review, CRF** Students answer end-of-section vocabulary, key ideas, math, and critical thinking questions. (**GENERAL**)

_ **Section Quiz, CRF** Students answer 6 objective questions about sedimentary rock. (**GENERAL**)

Lesson Plan

Section: Metamorphic Rock

Pacing

Regular Schedule:	**with lab(s):** N/A	**without lab(s):** 1 day
Block Schedule:	**with lab(s):** N/A	**without lab(s):** 0.5 day

Objectives

1. Describe two ways a rock can undergo metamorphism.

2. Explain how the mineral composition of rocks changes as the rocks undergo metamorphism.

3. Describe the difference between foliated and nonfoliated metamorphic rock.

4. Explain how metamorphic rock structures are related to deformation.

National Science Education Standards Covered

SAI 1 Abilities necessary to do scientific inquiry

SAI 2 Understandings about scientific inquiry

UCP 1 Systems, order, and organization

UCP 2 Evidence, models, and explanation

ES 1c Land forms are the result of a combination of constructive and destructive forces. Constructive forces include crustal deformation, volcanic eruption, and deposition of sediment, while destructive forces include weathering and erosion.

KEY
SE = Student Edition **TE** = Teacher's Edition
CRF = Chapter Resource File

FOCUS (*5 minutes*)

_ **Bellringer, TE** Ask students to write a description of how cookies are made and have them compare the process to how metamorphic rock is formed. **(GENERAL)**

_ **Bellringer Transparency** Use this transparency as students enter the classroom and find their seats.

MOTIVATE (*10 minutes*)

_ **Activity, Modeling Metamorphism, TE** Have students use modeling clay to learn how intense pressure and heat can cause rock to behave in similar ways. **(GENERAL)**

TEACH *(20 minutes)*

_ **Reading Strategy, SE** Have students write down any questions they may have while they read the section.

_ **Using the Figure, Analogies, TE** Have students think about and discuss analogies for regional and contact metamorphism. **(BASIC)**

_ **Research, Metamorphic Minerals, TE** Students research metamorphic minerals and create posters illustrating how the mineral is formed and what its uses are. **(GENERAL)**

_ **Discussion, Predicting Patterns, TE** Have students observe foliated and nonfoliated rock and predict what the terms foliated and nonfoliated mean before they read the appropriate section. **(BASIC)**

_ **Connection Activity, Real World, Asbestos Removal, TE** Have students find out about the uses of asbestos and any cleanup projects in their area. **(ADVANCED)**

_ **Homework, Making Models, TE** Have students make a model cross section of the Earth's crust. **(General)**

_ **Inclusion Strategies, TE** Have students conduct a scavenger hunt in their classroom to identify minerals that are used to make items that we use every day.

_ **Directed Reading, A/B, CRF** These worksheets reinforce basic concepts and vocabulary presented in the lesson. **(BASIC/SPECIAL NEEDS)**

_ **Vocabulary and Section Summary, CRF** Students write definitions of key terms and read a summary of section content. **(GENERAL)**

_ **Reinforcement Worksheet, CRF** This worksheet reinforces key concepts in the chapter. **(GENERAL)**

_ **Critical Thinking, CRF** Ask students to fill out the worksheet about how different rocks and gems are formed. **(GENERAL)**

_ **QuickLab, CRF** Students learn about contact and regional metamorphism using plastic play putty. **(GENERAL)**

CLOSE *(10 minutes)*

_ **Reteaching, Creating an Outline, TE** Students make an outline of the process involved in the formation of either foliated or nonfoliated rock. **(BASIC)**

_ **Quiz, TE** Students answer 2 questions about metamorphic rock. **(GENERAL)**

_ **Alternative Assessment, Preparing a Lesson, TE** Students prepare a lesson about this chapter for a second grade class. **(GENERAL)**

_ **Homework, Investigate Your Area, TE** Students search their town to discover the different ways rocks have been used in buildings and other structures. **(ADVANCED)**

_ **Section Review, CRF** Students answer end-of-section vocabulary, key ideas, math and critical thinking questions. **(GENERAL)**

_ **Section Quiz, CRF** Students answer 6 objective questions about metamorphic rock. **(GENERAL)**

Lesson Plan

End of Chapter Review and Assessment

Pacing

Regular Schedule: **with lab(s):** N/A   **without lab(s):** 2 days
Block Schedule: **with lab(s):** N/A   **without lab(s):** 1 day

---

KEY
SE = Student Edition   **TE** = Teacher's Edition
CRF = Chapter Resource File

_ **Chapter Review, CRF** Students answer end-of-chapter vocabulary, key ideas, critical thinking, and graphics questions. (**GENERAL**)

_ **Vocabulary Activity, CRF** Students review chapter vocabulary terms by completing a puzzle. (**GENERAL**)

_ **Concept Mapping Transparency, TE** Use this graphic to help students review key concepts.

_ **Chapter Test A/B/C, CRF** Assign questions from the appropriate test for chapter assessment. (**GENERAL/ADVANCED/SPECIAL NEEDS**)

_ **Performance-Based Assessment, CRF** Assign this activity for general level assessment for the chapter. (**GENERAL**)

_ **Standardized Test Preparation, CRF** Students answer reading comprehensions, math, and interpreting graphics questions in the format of a standardized test. (**GENERAL**)

_ **Test Generator, One-Stop Planner.** Create a customized homework assessment, quiz, or test using the HRW Test Generator program.

_ **CNN Video, CNN Presents Science in the News:** Scientists in Action, Segment 6, "Meteor Collision Geologist"

Rocks: Mineral Mixtures

MULTIPLE CHOICE

1. Which of the following rocks is not normally used as a construction material?
   a. marble
   b. halite
   c. limestone
   d. granite

   Answer: B   Difficulty: 1   Section: 1   Objective: 1

2. Which of the following processes changes rock on Earth's surface?
   a. metamorphism
   b. erosion
   c. compaction
   d. cementation

   Answer: D   Difficulty: 1   Section: 1   Objective: 3

3. When sedimentary rock is exposed to heat and pressure, what does it change into?
   a. magma
   b. igneous rock
   c. sedimentary rock
   d. metamorphic rock

   Answer: D   Difficulty: 1   Section: 1   Objective: 3

4. Scientists classify rocks
   a. by composition and texture.
   b. by volume.
   c. by mass.
   d. by color and size.

   Answer: A   Difficulty: 1   Section: 1   Objective: 4

5. Which of the following are ways magma is formed?
   a. by compaction and cementation
   b. by melting and cooling
   c. by changes in composition
   d. by weathering and erosion

   Answer: C   Difficulty: 1   Section: 2   Objective: 2

6. What kind of texture does igneous rock have when magma cools slowly?
   a. coarse-grained
   b. large-grained
   c. fine-grained
   d. medium-grained

   Answer: A   Difficulty: 1   Section: 2   Objective: 3

7. What kind of texture does igneous rock have when magma cools rapidly?
   a. coarse-grained
   b. medium-grained
   c. large-grained
   d. fine-grained

   Answer: D   Difficulty: 1   Section: 2   Objective: 3

8. What kind of rock is formed when magma intrudes into other rock?
   a. extrusive igneous rock
   b. metamorphic rock
   c. intrusive igneous rock
   d. organic sedimentary rock

   Answer: C   Difficulty: 1   Section: 2   Objective: 3

9. What kind of rock is formed from lava that cools on the Earth's surface?
   a. organic sedimentary rock
   b. metamorphic rock
   c. intrusive igneous rock
   d. extrusive igneous rock

   Answer: D   Difficulty: 1   Section: 3   Objective: 3

10. Which process forms sediment?
    a. weathering
    b. cementation
    c. compaction
    d. deposition

    Answer: A   Difficulty: 1   Section: 4   Objective: 1

11. What are strata?
    a. mineral fragments
    b. minerals crystallized out of solution
    c. layers in sedimentary rock
    d. fossils in sedimentary rock

    Answer: C   Difficulty: 1   Section: 4   Objective: 2

12. What kind of sedimentary rock can be cemented together by calcite or quartz?
    a. organic
    b. stratified
    c. chemical
    d. clastic
    Answer: D   Difficulty: 1   Section: 3   Objective: 2

13. What kind of sedimentary rock is made from dissolved minerals?
    a. organic
    b. chemical
    c. stratified
    d. clastic
    Answer: B   Difficulty: 1   Section: 3   Objective: 2

14. What kind of sedimentary rock is made from fossils?
    a. organic
    b. stratified
    c. chemical
    d. clastic
    Answer: A   Difficulty: 1   Section: 3   Objective: 3

15. What is the process called in which sedimentary rocks are arranged in layers?
    a. erosion
    b. extrusion
    c. weathering
    d. stratification
    Answer: D   Difficulty: 1   Section: 3   Objective: 3

16. How did humans use rocks in the past?
    a. to play sports
    b. to tell time
    c. to write
    d. to make tools
    Answer: D   Difficulty: 1   Section: 1   Objective: 1

17. Which of the following does NOT cause magma to form?
    a. an increase in pressure on rock
    b. a rise in temperature in rock
    c. a change in composition in rock
    d. a decrease in pressure on rock
    Answer: A   Difficulty: 1   Section: 2   Objective: 2

18. Sedimentary rock is formed through the process of
    a. cementation
    b. stratification.
    c. erosion.
    d. foliation.
    Answer: A   Difficulty: 1   Section: 3   Objective: 1

19. What has to increase for metamorphism to occur?
    a. weathering and erosion
    b. temperature and pressure
    c. melting and cooling
    d. compaction and cementation
    Answer: B   Difficulty: 1   Section: 4   Objective: 1

20. Besides weathering and erosion, what other forces shape the Earth's features?
    a. deposition and uplift
    b. exfoliation and foliation
    c. cementation and melting
    d. composition and texture
    Answer: A   Difficulty: 1   Section: 1   Objective: 2

21. When magma cools quickly, what kind of texture does rock have?
    a. coarse-grained
    b. large-grained
    c. medium-grained
    d. fine-grained
    Answer: D   Difficulty: 1   Section: 2   Objective: 2

22. What are the main categories of sedimentary rock?
    a. extrusive and intrusive
    b. clastic, chemical, and organic
    c. felsic and mafic
    d. foliated and nonfoliated
    Answer: B   Difficulty: 1   Section: 3   Objective: 2

23. When temperature and pressure change, what can happen to the minerals in rocks?
    a. They stay the same.
    b. They fragment and loosen.
    c. They bind closer together.
    d. They change into other minerals.
    Answer: D   Difficulty: 1   Section: 4   Objective: 2

24. During the rock cycle, what forms when magma cools?
    a. igneous rock
    b. sedimentary rock
    c. metamorphic rock
    d. foliated rock

    Answer: A   Difficulty: 1   Section: 2   Objective: 3

25. What do scientists call the rock that is formed when magma cools below the Earth's surface?
    a. extrusive igneous rock
    b. intrusive igneous rock
    c. eruptive rock
    d. volcanic rock

    Answer: B   Difficulty: 1   Section: 2   Objective: 3

26. Besides clastic and chemical, what is the other kind of sedimentary rock?
    a. extrusive
    b. foliated
    c. organic
    d. intrusive

    Answer: C   Difficulty: 1   Section: 4   Objective: 3

27. What kind of metamorphic rock has its mineral grains arranged in planes or bands?
    a. extrusive
    b. foliated
    c. nonfoliated
    d. intrusive

    Answer: B   Difficulty: 1   Section: 4   Objective: 3

28. Besides texture, how else are rocks classified?
    a. by the amount of foliation
    b. by their grain size
    c. by their grain shape
    d. by their composition

    Answer: D   Difficulty: 1   Section: 1   Objective: 4

29. The process in which rocks change shape is called
    a. deformation.
    b. deposition.
    c. composition.
    d. foliation.

    Answer: A   Difficulty: 1   Section: 4   Objective: 4

30. The process in which sediment is dropped and comes to rest is called
    a. deposition.
    b. stratification.
    c. cementation.
    d. foliation.

    Answer: A   Difficulty: 1   Section: 3   Objective: 2

31. Which of the following is a coarse-grained igneous rock?
    a. shale
    b. marble
    c. granite
    d. gneiss

    Answer: C   Difficulty: 1   Section: 2   Objective: 2

32. Partially decomposed plant material forms
    a. chemical sedimentary rock.
    b. fossiliferous limestone.
    c. clastic sedimentary rock.
    d. coal.

    Answer: D   Difficulty: 1   Section: 3   Objective: 3

33. When shale is exposed to slight heat and pressure, what foliated metamorphic rock does it become?
    a. schist
    b. gneiss
    c. phyllite
    d. slate

    Answer: D   Difficulty: 1   Section: 4   Objective: 3

34. Which rock was used to construct the pyramids at Giza?
    a. granite
    b. marble
    c. slate
    d. limestone

    Answer: D   Difficulty: 1   Section: 2   Objective: 1

35. What is the grain of igneous rock formed when magma cools quickly?
    a. fine-grained
    b. large-grained
    c. medium-grained
    d. coarse-grained

    Answer: A   Difficulty: 1   Section: 2   Objective: 3

36. How does clastic sedimentary rock begin?
    a. as magma
    b. as plant remains
    c. as fragments of rock
    d. as animal remains

    Answer: C   Difficulty: 1   Section: 3   Objective: 1

37. What do bends or folds in rocks show?
    a. They have been weathered.
    b. They have been deformed.
    c. They have cooled slowly.
    d. They have cooled rapidly.

    Answer: B   Difficulty: 1   Section: 4   Objective: 4

38. Besides being classified by their composition, how else are rocks classified?
    a. by their texture
    b. by their mass
    c. by their color
    d. by their volume

    Answer: A   Difficulty: 1   Section: 1   Objective: 4

39. What occurs when temperature and pressure inside the Earth's crust change?
    a. stratification
    b. deformation
    c. deposition
    d. metamorphism

    Answer: D   Difficulty: 1   Section: 4   Objective: 2

40. What is one way that magma forms?
    a. when rock is heated
    b. when rock is cooled
    c. when rock is cemented
    d. when rock is weathered

    Answer: A   Difficulty: 1   Section: 2   Objective: 1

41. What are the layers of sedimentary rock called?
    a. sediment
    b. strata
    c. clasts
    d. folds

    Answer: B   Difficulty: 1   Section: 3   Objective: 2

42. What is it called when sediment is dropped and comes to rest?
    a. erosion
    b. deposition
    c. weathering
    d. compaction

    Answer: B   Difficulty: 1   Section: 1   Objective: 2

43. What forces change a sedimentary rock into a metamorphic rock?
    a. heat and pressure
    b. weathering and erosion
    c. melting
    d. cooling

    Answer: A   Difficulty: 1   Section: 1   Objective: 3

44. What does all igneous rock begin as?
    a. crystals
    b. magma
    c. fissures
    d. mud cracks

    Answer: B   Difficulty: 1   Section: 2   Objective: 1

45. What can some organic sedimentary rocks can be made of?
    a. seaweed
    b. insects
    c. fossils
    d. living plants

    Answer: C   Difficulty: 1   Section: 3   Objective: 2

46. Besides heat, what else causes a rock to undergo metamorphism?
    a. melting
    b. weathering
    c. cooling rate
    d. pressure

    Answer: D   Difficulty: 1   Section: 4   Objective: 1

47. If wind in a desert suddenly blew all the time, what kind of rock would not form?
    a. metamorphic rock
    b. sedimentary rock
    c. organic sedimentary rock
    d. igneous rock
    Answer: B   Difficulty: 2   Section: 3   Objective: 2

48. If oceans become so polluted that corals are unable to form, what rock would not be able to form?
    a. clastic rock
    b. sedimentary rock
    c. organic sedimentary rock
    d. chemical rock
    Answer: C   Difficulty: 2   Section: 3   Objective: 2

49. Which of the following describes the process by which sediment drops and comes to rest?
    a. erosion
    b. deposition
    c. cementation
    d. melting
    Answer: deposition   Difficulty: 1   Section: 3   Objective: 2

50. Mud cracks form when fine-grained sediments are exposed to the air and
    a. evaporate.
    b. get wet.
    c. combine.
    d. dry out.
    Answer: D   Difficulty: 1   Section: 3   Objective: 3

51. What is the largest of all intrusive igneous rock formations?
    a. plutons
    b. fissures
    c. batholiths
    d. sills
    Answer: C   Difficulty: 1   Section: 2   Objective: 3

52. What does lava flow out of on the Earth's surface?
    a. fissures
    b. plateaus
    c. plutons
    d. ripple marks
    Answer: A   Difficulty: 1   Section: 2   Objective: 3

53. What kind of texture will a conglomerate rock have?
    a. large-grained
    b. fine-grained
    c. medium-grained
    d. coarse-grained
    Answer: D   Difficulty: 1   Section: 1   Objective: 4

54. What determines the composition of a rock?
    a. texture it has
    b. deposition that occurs
    c. minerals it is made of
    d. weathering of nearby rocks
    Answer: C   Difficulty: 1   Section: 1   Objective: 4

COMPLETION

Use the terms from the following list to complete the sentences below.

stratification	composition
rock cycle	rock
nonfoliated rock	erosion
gradient	strata
deposition	

55. The process in which layers of sedimentary rock are formed is called

    _______________________.
    Answer: stratification
                        Difficulty: 1   Section: 3   Objective: 3

56. A rock whose mineral grains are NOT formed in bands is called _______________________.
    Answer: nonfoliated rock
                        Difficulty: 1   Section: 4   Objective: 3

57. Grains of sand are washed into rivers and oceans through the process of
_______________.
    Answer: erosion   Difficulty: 1   Section: 1   Objective: 2

58. The minerals found in a rock determine its _______________.
    Answer: composition
                        Difficulty: 1   Section: 1   Objective: 4

59. Rocks change their composition during the _______________.
    Answer: rock cycle   Difficulty: 1   Section: 1   Objective: 2

Use the terms from the following list to complete the sentences below.

    stratification   index minerals
    intrusive igneous rock   uplift
    erosion

60. Weathering, erosion, deposition, and _______________ are the processes that shape
the Earth's surface.
    Answer: uplift   Difficulty: 1   Section: 1   Objective: 2

61. The process in which sedimentary rocks are arranged in layers is called
_______________.
    Answer: stratification
                        Difficulty: 1   Section: 3   Objective: 3

62. Minerals used to estimate temperature and pressure at which rock changes are called
_______________.
    Answer: index minerals
                        Difficulty: 1   Section: 4   Objective: 2

63. On the Earth's surface, weathering and _______________ make rock fragments.
    Answer: erosion   Difficulty: 1   Section: 2   Objective: 2

64. Rock formed from magma that cools below the earth's surface is _______________.
    Answer: intrusive igneous rock
                        Difficulty: 1   Section: 2   Objective: 3

Use the terms from the following list to complete the sentence below.

    extrusive   belsic
    mafic   clastic
    intrusive   felsic

65. The three types of sedimentary rock are: chemical, organic and _______________.
    Answer: clastic   Difficulty: 1   Section: 3   Objective: 2

Use the terms from the following list to complete the sentence below.

    sometimes   occasionally
    continually   periodically
    annually   biennially

66. The rock cycle happens _______________.
    Answer: continually Difficulty: 1   Section: 1   Objective: 1

Use the terms from the following list to complete the sentence below.

    recrystallizes   dissolves
    crystallizes   materializes
    synthesizes   actualizes

67. Salt is formed when halite in ocean water _______________.
    Answer: crystallizes Difficulty: 1   Section: 3   Objective: 1

SHORT ANSWER

69. How is clastic sedimentary rock different from chemical sedimentary rock?

    Answer:
    Answers will vary. Sample answer: Clastic sedimentary rock is formed from rock fragments that are cemented together by calcite or quartz. Chemical sedimentary rock is made of dissolved minerals that eventually crystallize.

    Difficulty: 2   Section: 3   Objective: 2

70. Describe how contact metamorphism is different from regional metamorphism.

    Answer:
    Answers will vary. Sample answer: Contact metamorphism occurs when magma comes into direct contact with rock. Regional metamorphism occurs when large pieces of the Earth's crust collide with each other.

    Difficulty: 2   Section: 4   Objective: 1

71. What will a nonfoliated rock look like under a microscope?

    Answer:
    Answers will vary. Sample answer: Under a microscope a nonfoliated rock will not have mineral grains that are aligned.

    Difficulty: 2   Section: 4   Objective: 3

72. How does limestone form?

    Answer:
    Answers will vary. Sample answer: Limestone is formed from the remains, or fossils, of animals that once lived in the ocean.

    Difficulty: 2   Section: 4   Objective: 2

73 How do rocks recrystallize?

    Answer:
    Answers will vary. Sample answer: Rocks recrystallize when the crystals of the minerals change in composition.

    Difficulty: 1   Section: 4   Objective: 2

74. Uplift and weathering are two of the processes that shape the features of the Earth. How are they different and how are they similar?

    Answer:
    Uplift is something that occurs as a result of activity underneath the Earth's surface. Weathering is a process that happens to the Earth's surface from its atmosphere—it is not an internal process. Both processes, however, change the physical surface of the Earth.

    Difficulty: 3   Section: 1   Objective: 2

75. You are walking on land where a volcano was once active. You pick up a rock that is smooth and appears to have no crystals. How do you think this rock was formed?

    Answer:
    The rock is an extrusive igneous rock that was made from lava and that cooled very quickly.

    Difficulty: 3   Section: 2   Objective: 4

76. What is the difference between composition and texture?

    Answer:
    Composition is the minerals of which a rock is made. Texture is the appearance of the rock based on the arrangement of the minerals from which it is made.

    Difficulty: 2   Section: 1   Objective: 4

77. How does the rate at which magma cools affect its texture?

Answer:
The more time magma has to cool, the larger its crystals are. If magma cools quickly, its crystals are very small or hardly even visible.

Difficulty: 1 Section: 2 Objective: 2

78. How can you tell if a rock is a sedimentary rock and not a nonfoliated metamorphic rock like quartzite?

Answer:
A sedimentary rock may have layers, while quartzite will not have layers but have a shiny, glittery appearance.

Difficulty: 2 Section: 3 Objective: 1

79. What is the difference between deformation and stratification?

Answer:
Stratification will appear in layers. It is the process by which sediment is laid down layer by layer. Deformation will not be in layers, but will appear in folds and bends in the rock.

Difficulty: 2 Section: 4 Objective: 4

80. Imagine you need to make a tool from a very large rock. You can choose between a foliated rock and a nonfoliated rock. Which would you choose and why?

Answer:
Because the foliated rock is arranged in bands, it would probably be easier to break.

Difficulty: 3 Section: 4 Objective: 3

81. What happens in the process of stratification?

Answer: Stratification is the process by which sediment is laid down layer after layer.

Difficulty: 1 Section: 3 Objective: 1

82. Describe the difference between how foliated and nonfoliated rock are formed.

Answer:
When heat and pressure are applied to certain metamorphic rock, if the minerals do not change, the minerals align and are arranged in layers. In nonfoliated rock the minerals change their composition and are recrystallized.

Difficulty: 2 Section: 4 Objective: 3

83. List four processes that change rock from one type to another.

Answer: weathering, changes in pressure, melting, and cooling

Difficulty: 1 Section: 1 Objective: 1

84. What are the three main classes of rock?

Answer: igneous, sedimentary, and metamorphic

Difficulty: 1 Section: 1 Objective: 2

85. How is a brick similar to a metamorphic rock?

Answer:
Bricks are made from clay and are baked to make them strong and resistant to weathering. Bricks are "metamorphosed" because they have different properties than dried clay.

Difficulty: 1 Section: 1 Objective: 4

86. Describe felsic and mafic rocks, and list three elements that occur in each type of rock.

Answer:
Felsic rock is lighter in color and weight and is rich in aluminum, silicon, sodium and potassium. Mafic rock is darker and heavier and is rich in iron, magnesium, and calcium.

Difficulty: 1 Section: 2 Objective: 2

87. What is a fissure?

    Answer:

    A fissure is a long crack in the Earth's crust through which lava erupts and flows.

    Difficulty: 1   Section: 2   Objective: 3

88. How does halite form?

    Answer:

    It forms when sodium ions become so concentrated in ocean water that halite crystallizes out of the water.

    Difficulty: 1   Section: 3   Objective: 2

89. What is stratification, and why is it important to Earth scientists?

    Answer:

    Stratification is the layering of rock. It is important because it records many events in Earth's history as well as erosion and deposition rates.

    Difficulty: 2   Section: 3   Objective: 3

90. Explain what a regionally metamorphosed rock is.

    Answer:

    A regionally metamorphosed rock has been changed by intense pressure and heat across great regions of the crust rather than by direct contact.

    Difficulty: 1   Section: 4   Objective: 1

91. What does composition of a metamorphic rock tell you about the rock's origin and formation?

    Answer:

    Different metamorphic minerals indicate the temperature and pressure conditions that existed when rock formed.

    Difficulty: 2   Section: 4   Objective: 2

ESSAY QUESTIONS

92. Why is rock a good building material?

    Answer:

    Rocks like granite and marble are good building materials because they can withstand weathering for long periods of time.

    Difficulty: 3   Section: 4   Objective: 2

93. What does an extrusive rock formation tell about what is going on below the Earth's surface?

    Answer:

    Answers will vary. Sample answer: An extrusive rock formation reveals that there is a lot of activity, perhaps volcanic, going on below the Earth's surface.

    Difficulty: 3   Section: 2   Objective: 3

94. Why is sedimentary rock more common on Earth's surface that metamorphic rock or igneous rock?

    Answer:

    All three rock types weather when they are uplifted to the Earth's surface, forming sediments that cover the Earth's surface.

    Difficulty: 3   Section: 1   Objective: 2

95. Early humans used rocks as tools to make other things as well as to construct buildings. Why was it better for them to use rocks than another material such as wood?

    Answer:
     Students' essays should elaborate on the properties of rocks—their hardness and ability to last over time as compared to wood, which would more easily decompose. Essays might also include that because of rock's properties they can easily shape other materials.

    Difficulty: 3   Section: 1   Objective: 1

MATCHING

a. composition	d. texture
b. rock	e. rock cycle
c. erosion	f. deposition

96. ____ solid mixture of crystals or one or more minerals

    Answer: B   Difficulty: 1   Section: 1   Objective: 2

97. ____ process by which new rock forms from old rock

    Answer: E   Difficulty: 1   Section: 1   Objective: 2

98. ____ process by which sediment is removed from its source

    Answer: C   Difficulty: 1   Section: 1   Objective: 2

99. ____ process by which sediment is dropped and comes to rest

    Answer: F   Difficulty: 1   Section: 1   Objective: 2

100. ____ the chemical makeup of a rock

    Answer: A   Difficulty: 1   Section: 1   Objective: 1

101. ____ size, shape, and position of grains that make up a rock

    Answer: D   Difficulty: 1   Section: 1   Objective: 4

a. foliated	d. deformation
b. pressure	e. nonfoliated
c. recrystallization	f. regional metamorphism

102. ____ process other than heat that causes metamorphism

    Answer: B   Difficulty: 1   Section: 4   Objective: 1

103. ____ process in which crystals in minerals change in size or composition

    Answer: C   Difficulty: 1   Section: 4   Objective: 2

104. ____ metamorphic rock in which mineral grains are not arranged in planes or bands

    Answer: E   Difficulty: 1   Section: 4   Objective: 3

105. ____ a change in the shape of rock caused by force

    Answer: D   Difficulty: 1   Section: 4   Objective: 4

106. ____ metamorphic rock in which mineral grains are arranged in bands

    Answer: A   Difficulty: 1   Section: 4   Objective: 3

107. ____ result of large pieces of rock deep within the Earth's crust colliding

    Answer: F   Difficulty: 1   Section: 4   Objective: 1

a. deposition	d. texture
b. erosion	e. rock cycle
c. rock	f. composition

108. ____ naturally occurring solid mixture of crystals of one or more minerals

    Answer: C   Difficulty: 1   Section: 1   Objective: 4

109. ____ process in which sediment is dropped and comes to rest

    Answer: A   Difficulty: 1   Section: 1   Objective: 2

110. ____ process by which new rock is made from old rock

    Answer: E   Difficulty: 1   Section: 1   Objective: 2

111. ____ the quality of a rock based on size and shape
   Answer: D   Difficulty: 1   Section: 1   Objective: 2
112. ____ process by which sediment is removed from its source
   Answer: B   Difficulty: 1   Section: 1   Objective: 2
113. ____ the chemical makeup of a rock
   Answer: F   Difficulty: 1   Section: 1   Objective: 4

   a. stratification   d. strata
   b. nonfoliated   e. intrusive igneous rock
   c. extrusive igneous rock

114. ____ metamorphic rock in which mineral grains are not arranged in bands
   Answer: B   Difficulty: 1   Section: 4   Objective: 3
115. ____ layers found in sedimentary rocks
   Answer: D   Difficulty: 1   Section: 3   Objective: 2
116. ____ rock that cools at the Earth's surface
   Answer: C   Difficulty: 1   Section: 2   Objective: 3
117. ____ process in which layers in sedimentary rock are formed
   Answer: A   Difficulty: 1   Section: 3   Objective: 1
118. ____ rock that cools below the Earth's surface
   Answer: E   Difficulty: 1   Section: 3   Objective: 2

   a. organic sedimentary rock   c. foliated rock
   b. extrusive igneous rock   d. rock cycle

119. ____ the process by which new rock forms from old rocks
   Answer: D   Difficulty: 1   Section: 1   Objective: 3
120. ____ igneous rock that cools on the Earth's surface
   Answer: B   Difficulty: 1   Section: 2   Objective: 3
121. ____ rocks made from animal or plant remains
   Answer: A   Difficulty: 1   Section: 3   Objective: 1
122. ____ metamorphic rocks in which mineral grains are arranged in bands
   Answer: C   Difficulty: 1   Section: 4   Objective: 3

CONCEPT MAPPING

123. Complete the concept map below using the following terms:

conglomerate
dikes
erode
composition

igneous rock
texture
sedimentary rock

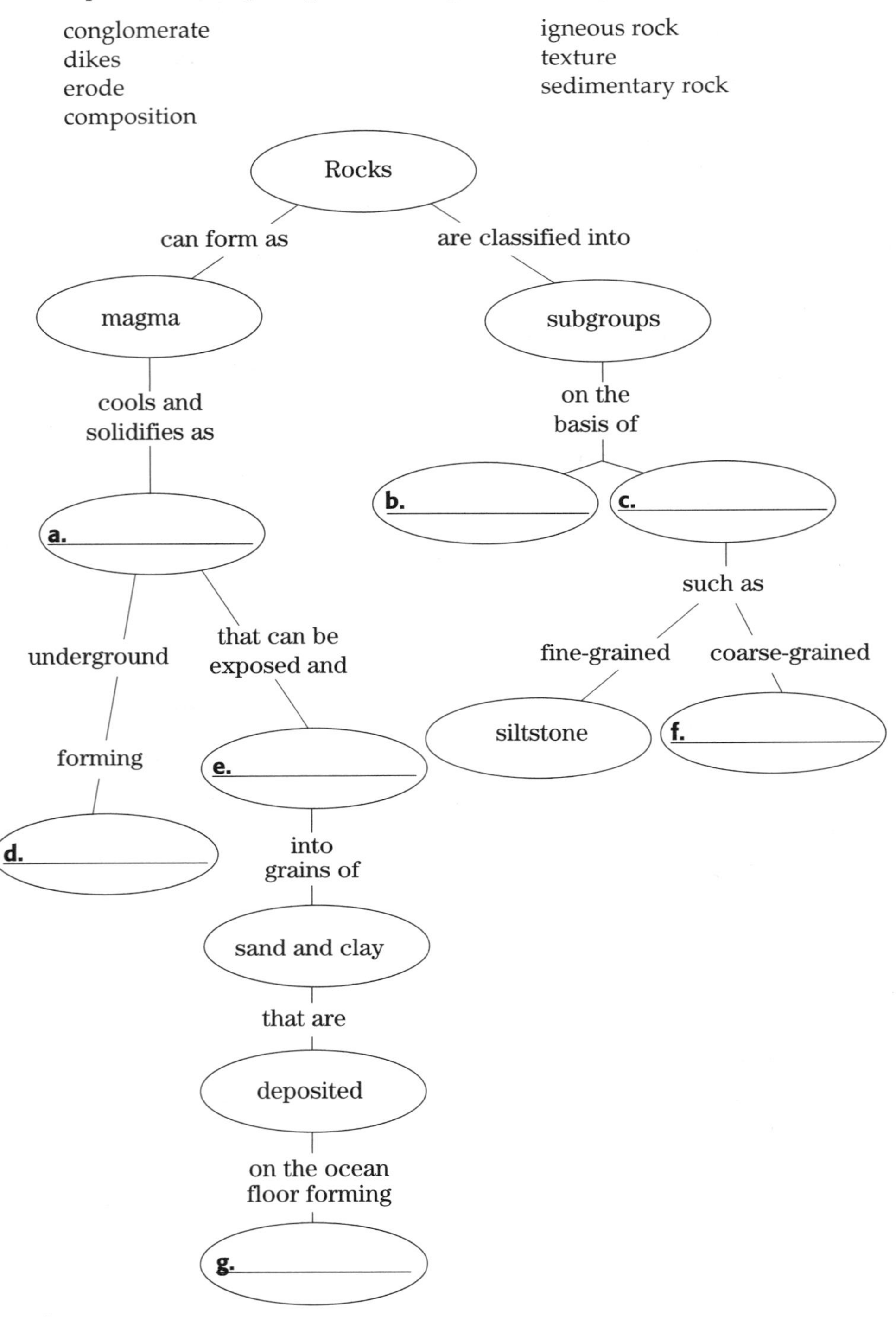

Answer:
a. igneous rock, b. composition, c. texture, d. dikes, e. erode, f. conglomerate, g. sedimentary rock

Difficulty: 2   Section: 4   Objective: 1